TELEVISION SCALES

Fig. 1. Hieronymus Bosch, *Ship of Fools* (1490–1500)

First published in 2019 by punctum books, Earth, Milky Way.
https://punctumbooks.com

ISBN-13: 978-1-950192-41-0 (print)
ISBN-13: 978-1-950192-42-7 (ePDF)

DOI: 10.21983/P3.0263.1.00

LCCN: 2019947001
Library of Congress Cataloging Data is available from the Library of Congress

Interior Design: Jocelyn Coreas-Romero, Skyler Depaoli, Karla Valverde, and Jasmine Vo
Cover Design: Vincent W.J. van Gerven Oei

HIC SVNT MONSTRA

NICK

SALVATO

TELEVISION

SCALES

Ⓟ

Contents

Acknowledgments

Cornell University's Society for the Humanities provided me with a travel grant that enabled a research trip to Los Angeles, described in this book's third chapter and coda. I thank the members of the Humanities Council and the Society's director, Paul Fleming, for their belief in and support of this project. Belief and support also came generously from the team at punctum books, including Eileen Joy and Vincent W.J. van Gerven Oei. It is a pleasure to undertake a project for a press that champions experimentation and risk-taking to the singular extent that punctum does.

During the years of working on *Television Scales,* I had a number of opportunities to share work in progress and benefited from the thoughtful feedback that interlocutors offered me on those occasions. Lindsay Brandon Hunter was a gracious host who invited me to give a lecture at the University at Buffalo, and her colleagues and students made the visit a memorable one with their smart conversation and good cheer. The annual gatherings of the Society for Cinema and Media Studies and Console-ing Passions are always fun and rewarding. Some of the friends with whom I get to talk about television at those conference meetings, like Hollis Griffin, Hunter Hargraves, and Andy Owens, are ones I almost only see once or twice a year; others work with me at Cornell, and I am grateful for the more sustained conversations I am able to enjoy with those friends, including Kriszta Pozsonyi, Samantha Sheppard, Sabine Haenni, and Amy Villarejo. Amy also deserves applause for her early encouragement of my idea to perform an eccentric version of television studies through a reckoning with Marilyn Strathern's writing. I likewise applaud Jeremy Braddock for leading Cornell's Media Studies Working Group, which formed while I was undertaking this project. Our group conversations are rich and varied, and I am sure that I have not fully appreciated all the oblique and subtle ways in which they have informed my work on this book.

I cannot name all the family members and chosen family members who support me, because I am lucky in their astonishing abundance. Some of them, like Richard Buggeln and Masha Raskolnikov, will encourage me to talk for hours and hours about my televisual and theoretical obsessions, an encouragement that keeps me on track and that spurs my thinking and writing. Others, like Carlynn Houghton, provide a counterpoised and welcome relief by chattering instead with me about animals, babies, and the other adored and adorable beings in whom we invest so much attention when we are not watching or thinking about television…or when we are. In Maria Fackler and Samuel Buggeln, I am fortunate and grateful beyond compare to have a respective best friend and husband who nurture both the focusing with me when needed and the releases from focus when it is important for release to come into play. As for Tessibel, to whom I perversely dedicate this book though he does not know what books are, he deserves the distinction nonetheless for all the purr- and cuddle-filled administrative assistance he provides. What he gives really is loving assistance, and the uncanniness with which he came into my life precisely at the time that I needed him more than I could have known (and onto my lap as I was composing this sentence) is a boon for which I am happy to embarrass myself by naming it here.

Introduction

The title of this book, *Television Scales,* invites itself to be apprehended in at least two ways: as a clause, in which the nominal subject, *television,* performs the action of the verbal predicate, *scales*; and as a phrase, in which the plural thing, *scales,* is described by the adjectival modifier, *television.* Like television itself, in some of its guises or incarnations, this observation about the dual, not quite split, meaning of *Television Scales* may be taken as pedestrian. Arguably — hopefully — more interesting (also like television, in others of its guises and incarnations) could be a meditation on the phenomenal gap or relay, at once intellective and affective, between cognizing first the clausal and then the phrasal meaning of *Television Scales,* or vice versa. In that opening, perhaps the flicker of imagistic, which is also to say imaginative, association is at play and at stake. Does the plural thing, *scales,* assert itself pictorially to consciousness as the scales of justice (and are those scales modified, descriptively, by holding one or two television monitors, either of the same size, balanced, or of different sizes, tipping the scales)...or are those scales thought and felt as the ones that take their place in our doctors' offices and on our bathroom floors, ready to weigh television for its heaviness here, its lightness there?...And then, as if at the zap of a remote-control device, do the scales themselves transform into televisions, the digital screen in which weight would be numbered now filled instead with the avatars of sitcoms and procedurals, the beam and pan refigured as boom and microphone, or the commanding arm and hand of network "brass"?

If this speculative conjuration of images and their transmutation works, then it will produce more than a set of rejected, because overly literal, candidates to appear on this book's cover. Rather, the spark that may ignite in the flip, as it were, from the clausal channel to the phrasal one, could be understood as a local manifestation of a more global paradox, whose exploration will animate this book and which I would describe, adopting and adapting language from the anthropologist Marilyn Strathern (stay tuned for more segments featuring her), as the simultaneity of scale maintenance and scale slippage. On the one hand, what I have just dubbed a semiotic "flip" sends us not only across registers of televisual meaning but also across the sizes, shapes, and scopes of that meaning's mattering — hence the slippage of scale. Yet on the other hand, in order to comprehend such slipping as slipping requires a more or less stable sense of the scale or scales that are being slipped — hence the maintenance of that scale or scales. The heuristic value of inhabiting this scalar paradox will, in its enfolding with other, allied strategies for regarding television at once aslant and head-on, obtain in and as a series of movements calibrated to be sometimes bigger, sometimes smaller, and sometimes scaled in between.

Before and behind the drive to motor such multiscalar movements, this book proceeds from the premise that the central, unresolved, and finally irresolvable challenges for television studies are indeed scalar ones: how to approach the vast archive of historical television materials, how to reckon with the staggering rate and volume of contemporary televisual output, and, most important, how to decide on a sound negotiation of the many different scales at which one may investigate the ontologically dense and variegated field that is "television." Where this last matter is concerned, I will now ask you to consider provisionally with me — before I gleefully dismantle it — a list of taxonomic registers for approaching television, each of which is both a quantitative and qualitative scale, and each of which is also unstable because of its internal and relational complexities.

One could assess television at the scale of its *medium of transmission* (but which? analog broadcast, analog cable, digital cable, satellite — and with what emplacement in larger transmedia ecologies?). One could assess television at the scale of *industry* (but, again, which of many industrial formations — and with what national or supranational coordinates?). One could assess television at the scale of *network* (what kind, in what market, with what regulatory oversight?); at the scale of *genre* (with what relationship to the logic of the programming grid, to what extends beyond the grid, to other genres?); at the scale of *series* (with what slot in the grid and beyond it, what consequent adjacencies to other programming, what generic affiliation, what syndication potential or actualization, what staff?); at the scale of *episode* (where in a series's run, what deviation from or conformity to series norms, what guest or nonce personnel?); and at so many more scales — not to speak of attempting to move critically through and across these scales and others. Indeed, my deliberately partial list does not even begin to take properly into account related work concerning the scales of television criticism (scholarly, journalistic, otherwise), the experience of viewership (casual, fan, and more), stardom and its others, changing reception technics, the sites of those technics' installation, the imbrication of these scaled phenomena — and on and on.

In the face of this scalar volatility, one could experience dizziness bordering on disorientation. One could also, as a number of thoughtful media scholars have done, take inspirational cues from DeLandian flat ontology, itself inspired by Deleuzian assemblage theory. Yet while flat ontologists can valuably claim that they reckon with and even push through the kinds of scalar problematics that I have charted here, the form that their reckoning takes produces, in my view, another (if you like, displaced) irresolvable challenge: how to address adequately the very real, material, and sometimes intransigent structures and hierarchies that limn the field of television — and that no level of sophistication in theorizing flatness can finally undo our need to recognize. Searching for a different and likely riskier way — one that would answer this concern — I take up ideas from a critical source to which I gestured above and that, unlike the DeLandian line, has so far had virtually no traction in media scholarship: the meta-critical writings of feminist, Melanesianist, and cultural anthropologist Marilyn Strathern and of her most thoughtful, recent commentators.

Strathern is probably best known, both within and beyond anthropology, for her influential, if also contested, 1988 book *The Gender of the Gift*, a monograph that draws extensively on her own fieldwork in Papua New Guinea and on the work of many other anthropologists who conducted later fieldwork at the same or related sites in the 1970s and 1980s. My own interest in Strathern pivots on work that she undertook in the period just following the publication of *The Gender of the Gift*, most notably the short book *Partial Connections*, in which Strathern grapples with unresolved challenges produced in her earlier work, including the limitations of a comparatist method, the problem of incommensurability, and — most important in the present context — the issue of scale and its relationship to complexity. Indeed, Strathern uses the occasion of writing *Partial Connections*, alongside allied, shorter texts like "The Relation" and "Environments Within," to put the problem of scale at the center of her meditations on method and field — and she does so in a fashion that, renewed and reoriented through the effort of translation, could yield a bold, unusual model for television studies' evolution.

To put it succinctly and summarily, Strathern's signal gesture is to risk what could, at first, look like a confusion of the object of analysis (in her case, the stuff of fieldwork) with its frame (the anthropological lens); in fact, her key contribution is to insist that frames are just as discursively constructed and culturally situated as objects, that objects may be just as pedagogical as the frames through which we tend to view them, that both objects and frames have irreducible complexities, and that the relations we can posit between objects and frames — or objects and objects, or frames and frames — are only ever *partial* (in both senses of that word). Yet admitting such partiality is the first step in the eking of a critical practice that generates real interest and surprising insight in a number of ways, including in the fastening onto objects that announce their framing of themselves and onto frames that announce their own object-status. Put another way, Strathern makes stunning connections among things that self-scale and scales that self-thingify. At the level of concretion indicated by this abstraction, Strathern pushes past the comparatist framework and collides things-as-scales (such as trees and flutes) with scales-as-things (including cyborg feminism and fractal theory) in order intensely to honor, yet also to understand intensively, the complexities of worlds. Moreover, within and across partial connections, Strathern can acknowledge instantiations of structure and hierarchy, yet she is not thereby compelled to reproduce them as she also takes stock of their dimensions, textures, and historical changeability — and, in this way, I take her to have developed a critical practice more responsible in its routes to and through partial connections than can be rendered in or as the more thoroughly deterritorializing assemblages of flat ontology.

For television studies, the implications of such work of Strathern's are thrilling. What could it mean to find, through a Strathernian approach, a rigorous, responsible — yet adventurous, weird — method through which not to compare but to connect items and, in so doing, to short-circuit the conservative or boring uses to which the standard television taxonomies, sketched above, may tend? Unfolding a complexly multipart answer to that question is the central endeavor of this book. Following this introduction's ensuing review of the extant deployments of scale as a concept, both implicit and explicit, in major works of television studies, and then segueing through a chapter-length reading of a few key texts by Strathern and her interlocutors, I offer that multipart answer in three further chapters: Chapter 2 will route its meditation on the scalar problematics of television through a consideration (that is, a careful yet creative undoing) of three binarisms through which we tend to understand both the production of television content and prevalent techniques for that content's reception: in/on, flip/flop, and binge/purge. Chapter 3 invokes (and complicates, bordering on dismantling) the various meanings of the word *scale* — weight, rule, map, interval, ladder — as it ekes partial, perhaps promiscuous connections among television materials that are usually weighed, ruled, mapped, and so forth in more pedestrian ways. Chapter 4 offers a close engagement with Dodie Bellamy's experimental book *The TV Sutras*; the engagement, among other effects, mimes *The TV Sutras*'s own formal experimentation, and it does so to prompt a (not merely punning) reckoning with television studies' *sutures,* where *suture* connotes — to borrow and repurpose two keywords for Strathern — both connection and cut. Then, elaborating on Strathern's preoccupation with what she calls "remainders," the book's coda will gesture toward what remains for television studies to explore on *Television Scales*'s unorthodox model, including a peripatetic critical practice that I cheekily call, "vulgar psychogeography."

* * *

To date, the most important work in media studies to make prominent the conceptualizations of scale is work not primarily or fundamentally trained, in its conceptualizations, on television. For instance, Mary Ann Doane — who has, in other contexts, made television a signal object of scrutiny — turns instead, in her meditations on and with scale, to filmic faciality and its rendering in that signature cinematic technique, the close-up. Arguing that "the close-up performs the inextricability of [...] two seemingly opposed formulations, simultaneously posing as both microcosm and macrocosm, detail and whole" — not only for the cinema but also for key texts in the history of cinema studies — Doane places her central emphasis on the putative contrast or opposition, which is in fact a critical interdependence, between "extensiveness, scale, an imposing stature, the awe of the gigantic" and "the charm of the miniature."[1] Further, she asserts that the capacity of the close-up to hold together and in tension these seemingly contrary characteristics — "both detail of a larger scene and totality in its own right — a spectacle of scale with its own integrity" — "responds to [a] need" that is "specific to modernity": namely, "strongly felt loss" in the face of "accelerating rationalization, specialization, and disintegration of the sense of a social totality," for which the close-up's claim to wholeness provides simulacral compensation and fantasmatic consolation.[2] Compelling in its endeavor to take stock of what remains more or less consistent about the status of the close-up across a range of national and historical contexts, Doane's argument has less pertinence for the study of television, in which the close-up and extreme close-up, though certainly deployed, are deployed with much less frequency than the medium close-up and medium shot, especially for the rendering of the human subject and yet more especially for the rendering of subjectivity as faciality. In films that make vital use of the close-up and the extreme close-up — and that have enjoyed a significant reception on large screens — the portion of the face's ambivalent appearance that aligns with a deterritorializing impulse may vividly align as well with the scale of monumentality and excess; its reterritorialization with the detailed, even miniaturizing, context against which the close-up performs, in Doane's words, its "extractability" and "uncontainab[ility]."[3] Yet in television, for the most part, the nuance and quality inhering in a given actorly *performance,* rather than the yielding up of that performance to the camera, will instead tend to be the locus, the instigator, for prompting "questions of inwardness [versus] exteriority," which may, as Noa Steimatsky asserts of mediated faciality (and in lan-

1   Mary Ann Doane, "The Close-Up: Scale and Detail in the Cinema," *differences* 14, no. 3 (2003): 89–111, at 93, 92.

2   Ibid., 93.

3   Ibid., 104.

guage similar to Doane's), "come into play as on a Möbius strip that belies their opposition."[4]

Of course, focusing attention on a particular technique, like the close-up, furnishes just one way among many to make the issue of scale central to the work of theorizing media and culture. Taking a more tentacular approach, media theorist Anna McCarthy, in a seminal meta-critical essay on the history and politics of cultural studies, "asks what the concept of scale means for methodology in cultural studies" and "propose[s] that a politics of scale has historically motivated cultural studies' interventions in the way knowledge is produced in the disciplines and spaces of higher education."[5] Tracking this history and its politics, McCarthy discloses how, in an ongoing, foundational way for cultural studies, orders of scale have determined the course of knowledge production and its disciplinary boundaries, supplied theories with their methods and the rationales for those methods, and also enabled critiques of methods deemed wanting. Or, as she puts it more wryly:

> You can attend a panel of world system historians in the morning and chide them for the absence of "voices" in their accounts, and then criticize a panel of ethnomethodologists and microhistorians for disregarding the big picture in the afternoon. In each instance, what you are calling for is an impossible thing: a research stance that affords a total view, and which is able to move effortlessly between scales.[6]

If this diagnosis seems not only wry but also grim, McCarthy pivots from the diagnosis to a more sanguine advocacy and finds value in sliding from "chid[ing]" to playfulness, in substituting for the impossibility of moving "effortlessly between

---

4   Noa Steimatsky, *The Face on Film* (New York: Oxford University Press, 2017), 21.

5   Anna McCarthy, "From the Ordinary to the Concrete: Cultural Studies and the Politics of Scale," in *Questions of Method in Cultural Studies,* eds. Mimi White and James Schwoch (Malden: Wiley-Blackwell, 2006), 21.

6   Ibid., 26.

scales" the supple possibilities afforded by moving accretively with and through them:

> The slippery relativism of orders of scale — always open to the possibility of adding one more degree of size or magnification, one more level of concreteness or abstraction, always producing continuities between things and ideas, between universals and the particulars that produce them — makes them highly heuristic thinking tools for cultural materialists.[7]

Laudable as it is to find "heuristic" worth in scalar play along these lines, I wonder nonetheless about how to push further — or at least in other directions and at other ranges than those on which McCarthy alights. That is, what if one established a yet more heterodox — and unorthodox — relationship (say, a Strathernian one) to scale, precisely to recognize and make a virtue of partial rather than "total view[s]," as well as to enable the not merely accretive but effortful, purposive, and reflexive movement between or among scales: scales re-thought or even undone (rescaled, un-scaled) in the enactment of such movement?

If television studies, as a subset of the broader terrain of media studies to which Doane and McCarthy are contributing, has not quite asked such a question of and with scale, the field may nonetheless be understood as constitutively shaped by scalar problematics — though the problematics have not always, or even often, been designated explicitly as scalar ones. Indeed, I would recognize scale in its form as (1) a structuring absence or *mute motor* — recognized only tacitly as a central problematic for grappling with and seeking to grasp television's ontology — as the first of five salient ways in which scale appears, or skirts appearance, in a body of texts either canonically constitutive of television studies or contributive to its contemporary vibrancy. Remaining ways of understanding scale's place in television studies include the (2) *metonymic,* when televisual conceptualizing obtains adjacent to — (almost but not quite) in

---

7   Ibid., 27.

identity with — the notion or language of scale; (3) *metaphoric,* when scale or, more likely, its rhetorical proximation is equated with or substituted for another problematic that it simultaneously renders legible and displaces; (4) *modular,* when a critic moves from (and, in so moving, articulates) one scale to another as a matter of method or for the contouring of argument; and (5) *monadic,* when a critic identifies one specific scale at which criticism should — or should not — proceed.

Though I can, in the present pages, only scale to snapshot my survey of these five tendencies in television studies, I ask you to see the gesture as, in McCarthy's words, "open to the possibility of adding [...] more," an additive procedure that, I warrant, would shore up the sense of scale's suffusing germaneness to the study of television. I am perhaps at the same time asking, via this snapshot, a version of Charlotte Brunsdon's 1998 question, "What Is the 'Television' of Television Studies?" In answering that question, Brunsdon manifests a paradigmatically representative version of tendency (1), as her identification of "three particular areas of interest in [...] television studies: the definition of the television text, the textual analysis of the representations of the social world offered therein, and the investigation of the television audience," does not name scale as an explicit referent but nonetheless discloses how working multiply across scales has given, at least, a tripartite "television" (which could have been defined and scaled otherwise) to the version or tradition of television studies (that is, humanistic rather than social scientific) that Brunsdon salutes and whose extenuation she models.[8] Further, one could say that Brunsdon is not only extenuating the scholarship but also its own, prior likelihood to make scale a structuring absence, a mute motor, of inquiry. (Without using the word *scale,* she nonetheless asks the discipline to scale *both* to the "production" of texts and to the "productivity" of those texts, *both* to "qualitative audience research" and to "working

---

8   Charlotte Brunsdon, "What Is the 'Television' of Television Studies?" in *The Television Studies Book,* eds. Christine Geraghty and David Lusted (New York: St. Martin's Press, 1998), 105.

with larger samples."[9]) When Brunsdon identifies "books such as Williams's *Television: Technology and Cultural Form* (1974) and John Fiske and John Hartley's *Reading Television* (1978)" as watershed efforts in the "hybrid" enunciation of television studies that she still finds, two decades later, "exciting," a meaningful portion of her excitement comes from the discipline's "dynamic potential" to continue to cross "boundaries" — and, while crossing boundaries thus, also to lay claim to a scale or scales for television studies.[10] Indeed, what but designating an "exciting" (if implicit) scale for the field — trans-episodically durational, crossing the slots of the programming grid — does Williams's *Television* accomplish when he theorizes "flow" as crucial to and generative of the 1970s television phenomenon?[11] (And what but rejecting that scale for another, in his view more proper one — yet once more, only implied rather than named as scale — does John Ellis retort when he calls for "segment" rather than flow to be comprehended as the essential unit or component of television's ontology?[12])

If 1974 was, to borrow and recast language from Brunsdon, an "inaugur[al]" and "originary" year for television studies, then not just Williams's book but also Horace Newcomb's *TV: The Most Popular Art* helps to account for that year's primacy to the field.[13] From its first, influential pages, Newcomb's book also manifests tendency (2), as it presents a suite of arguable metonyms for scale(s) — television's "range" making it "so much more than art," television involving the "multiple needs" of different subjects, television provoking "infinitely varied" "responses," and so forth — in order to describe and explain the interinanimating complexities that result in "[n]o one seem[ing] to know

9   Ibid., 110.

10 Brunsdon, "What Is the 'Television' of Television Studies?" 109–10.

11 Raymond Williams, *Television: Technology and Cultural Form* (New York: Routledge Classics, 2003), 69–120.

12 John Ellis, *Visible Fictions: Cinema, Television, Video,* revised edn. (New York: Routledge, 1992), 111–26.

13 Brunsdon, "What Is the 'Television' of Television Studies?" 109, 110.

just what the medium is."[14] Regarding the earliest seminal work by Fiske and Hartley, named by Brunsdon alongside Williams's pathbreaking book, there we may find a strong tendency — the third in my accounting — to metaphorize scale; as, for instance, when they "quest" after "the smallest signifying unit of code" in television programming and understand that particularly scaled unit to have a proportional, generalizing relationship both to the "world of television" *in toto* and to the "real social world" to which television, at its various scales, attaches symbolically (yet not only symbolically).[15]

Throughout the 1980s and 1990s, a second and third generation of critics building on, yet also departing from, the field-forming norms established by Williams, Newcomb, et al. — ones that I am calling *modular* in their scaling and rescaling — were also, crucially driving television studies to pay closer and deeper attention to such vectors of identity, sociality, and historicity as class, gender, ethnicity, race, and sexuality. So, for instance, we find Lynne Joyrich, in the feminist intervention of *Re-Viewing Reception,* rallying for the discipline to scale "down" and "in" from a focus on putatively universal subjects (in fact, default male subjects) to subjects gendered — within, by, and beyond television — as women.[16] Also guided by feminist methods and principles, Mimi White launches into *Tele-Advising* at the scale of the synecdoche; she uses an account of the sitcom ALF to model and modulate, as it were in miniature, what she will then continue to argue, at a variety of scales and across programming modes, regarding advising, advertising, confessing, and therapizing in the television landscape.[17] And in a more intersectional

14 Horace Newcomb, *TV: The Most Popular Art* (Garden City: Anchor Press/ Doubleday, 1974), 1.

15 John Fiske and John Hartley, *Reading Television* (London: Methuen, 1978), 65, 21.

16 Lynne Joyrich, *Re-Viewing Reception: Television, Gender, and Postmodern Culture* (Bloomington and Indianapolis: Indiana University Press, 1996), 3–20.

17 Mimi White, *Tele-Advising: Therapeutic Discourse in American Television* (Chapel Hill: The University of North Carolina Press, 1992), 1–24.

framework — coming on the heels of Patricia Mellencamp's recognition, in the introduction to the influential anthology *Logics
of Television,* that the volume appears "absent [...] any analysis
of the representation of race"[18] — Beretta E. Smith-Shomade asserts in *Shaded Lives* that, at the scales of demography, authority,
spectacularity, and more, not just women's lives and matters but
black women's lives and matters must be at the forefront of a television studies committed to industrial transformation, pedagogical reform, and social justice.[19]

Some contemporary work in television studies, while in-
debted to the modularity — and often as well to the identitarian
politics — of these precedential examples (and, again, they are
just a few illustrative examples among many others that could
be adduced) also exhibit what I have dubbed here the *monadic*
tendency in their scalar positioning. For instance, in *Ethereal
Queer: Television, Historicity, Desire,* Amy Villarejo uses a sly
footnote to remind us of her ongoing conviction that the scale
of close reading is incommensurate to a proper reckoning with
television's economic and industrial determinants and should
therefore be bracketed,[20] whereas Jeremy G. Butler devotes *Television Style* precisely to the obverse approach, using the scale of
close reading, as well as its recalibrations over the course of the
book, to guide each of its chapters' interpretive moves.[21]

Reflexive reengagements with most of the texts named
here — alongside other, coincident texts from the annals of television studies' history, to which they will become, as it were,
sutured — will constitute the portion of this book's final chapter
called, "The TV Studies Sutras." Among other agendas, efforts
to pave the way for how and why such reflexive reengagements

18 Patricia Mellencamp, "Prologue," in *Logics of Television: Essays in Cultural
   Criticism,* ed. Patricia Mellencamp (Bloomington and Indianapolis: Indiana University Press, 1990), 10.

19 Beretta E. Smith-Shomade, *Shaded Lives: African-American Women and
   Television* (New Brunswick: Rutgers University Press, 2002), 1–7.

20 Amy Villarejo, *Ethereal Queer: Television, Historicity, Desire* (Durham:
   Duke University Press, 2014), 182.

21 Jeremy G. Butler, *Television Style* (New York: Routledge, 2010).

should obtain in that chapter's semi-terminus, and with what relationship to the scalar business that is the book's chief *modus operandi*, will also be sutured to meditations on flipping and flopping, bingeing and purging, weighing and ruling, and more. Or, to put this meta-critical assertion another, Strathernian way, these efforts will star a series of *partial constellations*, a phrase meant both to echo and to ring a change on Strathern's title (and concept), *Partial Connections*. Admiring as I am of what Strathern accomplishes through the rubric of connecting — a multivalent accomplishment that I will unpack in the ensuing chapter of this book — I favor, for the most part, the rubric of constellating for the ways in which it may more fully and immediately index the multiplicity, as well as the simultaneity, of a variety of connections that the critic is poised to make. Indeed, it is a term favored by other scholars in television studies, some of them already cited above, who are likewise seeking to conjure a sense of such multiplicitous and simultaneous connections — as, for instance, when Villarejo writes of "the culture industries [...] emerg[ing] [...] in relation to those historical constellations of art, freedom, thought, and rationalization (or unfreedom) that calibrated Adorno's thought,"[22] or when Herman Gray writes of black racializations in American television that they come together as a "constellation of productions, histories, images, representations, and meanings associated with [a] black presence in the United States."[23] In line with such work and allied scholarly efforts, *Television Scales* offers its own constellations, in all of their avowed partiality, as further testament to messy medial complexities. Those complexities prompt at once the composing and the decomposing of our scales of critical understanding, and they also constitute whatever we, per Brunsdon, query as the "What?" of television studies' "television."

---

22 Amy Villarejo, "Adorno by the Pool; or, Television Then and Now," *Social Text* 34, no. 2 (2016): 71–87, at 73.

23 Herman Gray, *Watching Race: Television and the Struggle for Blackness* (Minneapolis: University of Minnesota Press, 2004), 12.

I

Strathern (in) Television

This chapter is comprised of two movements. In the first, longer part, I offer a close and sustained reading of a few key texts by Marilyn Strathern — *Partial Connections,* "The Relation," and "Environments Within" — and a related unpacking of a stunning, recent response to her theoretical work, Martin Holbraad and Morten Axel Pedersen's essay, "Planet M: The Intense Abstraction of Marilyn Strathern." I do so in order to lay further and fuller groundwork for a Strathernian approach to television studies, sketched more summarily in this book's "Introduction." Focusing on a deliberate and deliberative neologism, *abstension,* that propels Holbraad and Pedersen's extended gloss on Strathern, I introduce a nearly allied one of my own, *obstension,* and posit its interpretive value for scholarship. Then, in a second, shorter movement, I turn from the abstract to the concrete and home in on a couple of seemingly unrelated examples of television — ones that I connect partially, through obstension — in order to model in miniature and with specificity the kinds of work that my Strathernian model for television studies may galvanize, both in the remaining chapters of this book and beyond.

In the foreword to *Partial Connections,* Strathern indicates that she will address "[s]ome commonplace, persistent, but also interesting problems [...] in the organization of anthropological materials," and those "interesting problems" hinge, as she proceeds to elaborate, on questions of scale and complexity.[1] Let me quote a passage in which these two terms begin to acquire their thick salience for her study — and then ask us to submit the passage to a playful thought experiment:

[T]he question of complexity seems from one point of view a simple matter of scale. The more closely you look, the more detailed things are bound to become. Increase in one dimension (focus) increases the other (detail of data). For example, comparative questions that appear interesting at a distance, on closer inspection may well fragment into a host of subsidiary (and probably more interesting) questions. Complexity thus also comes to be perceived as an artefact of questions asked, and by the same token boundaries drawn: more complex questions produce more complex answers. Across Melanesia as a whole, it might seem intriguing to look, say, for the presence or absence of initiation practices. When one then starts examining specific sets of practices, it becomes obvious that "initiation" is no unitary phenomenon, and there appears to be as broad a gap between different initiatory practices as between the presence or absence of the practices themselves. As an effect of scale, all this might seem unremarkable. But it does, in fact, produce some trouble for the anthropological understanding of the phenomena in question.[2]

Why do "effect[s] of scale" that "seem," at first blush, to be "unremarkable" tend, if treated properly, to "produce some trouble" for anthropology? What this passage begins to intimate but does not yet spell out explicitly is that the "trouble" stems from the manner in which, in Strathern's view, *equivalent and irreducible levels of complexity* obtain — replicate, if you like — at every scale at which an anthropologist may wish to study phenomena. Now, the thought experiment: substitute the phrase *across tel-*

1   Marilyn Strathern, *Partial Connections,* updated edn. (New York: AltaMira Press, 2004), xiii.
2   Ibid., xiii–xiv.

evision as a whole for Strathern's, "Across Melanesia as a whole";
pick one or another key television phenomenon — *syndication,
advertising, documentary, cosmetic,* and so forth — to substitute
for "initiation"; and you may begin to discern how germane
Strathern's identification of "some trouble" may be to a television studies as sensitive to irreducible complexity, at a numerous variety of scales, as is her version of cultural anthropology
to the stuff of fieldwork.

Just a little later in the foreword, Strathern spells out more
plainly what is stake in thinking through the problem of repli-
cative complexity across differently scaled interpretive frameworks:

> It is conventional to imagine [...] scaling as a kind of branch-
> ing, as though one were dealing with a segmentary lineage
> system or a genealogical tree, where the more embracing or
> more remote orders contain derivative or recent ones. But
> the interesting feature about switching scale is not that one
> can forever classify into greater or lesser groupings but that
> *at every level complexity replicates itself in scale of detail.* "The
> same" order of information is repeated, eliciting equivalently
> complex conceptualization. While we might think that ideas
> and concepts grow from one another, each idea can also seem
> a complete universe with its own dimensions, as corrugated
> and involute as the last.[3]

According to Strathern's argument, complexity inheres in such
dimensions of phenomena, as well as in our conceptualizations
of these phenomena, as texturality and intrication (and, potentially, in intricate texturality) — hence her stunning introduction of the metaphorical language, "corrugated and involute"
to conjure a vivid and precise sense of the complexity that she
imagines. Moreover, scale's relationship to such "corrugated and
involute" complexity is *itself* complex — which is why, alongside
her adoption of one kind of metaphorical language ("corrugated

---

3   Ibid., xvi (emphasis added).

and involute"), she rejects another, less complex metaphor, that of the branching tree, as a way to account for scale's ontology and the epistemology that it ought to conduce. (As she charts elsewhere in the foreword, the metaphor of Cantor dust does better than that of the branching tree to proffer an accurate, salutary notion of scale's beings and doings.[4]) Having positioned scale, complexity, and their relationship to one another in this fashion, Strathern raises an implicit question that it remains for the body of *Partial Connections* to endeavor to answer: what should a scholar *do* methodologically with her materials, both descriptively and interpretively, once she has recognized the persnickety challenge that staggering complexity, asymptotically approaching infinity, may be recognized at each and every scale — that is, through each and every lens — with which the materials are apprehended? Unsurprisingly, the answer to the question is complex, polyvalent, and expressed across a number of more and less explicitly linked passages in a text that deliberately introduces "cuts" across which Strathern playfully, if also headily, invites the reader to jump with her.[5] Let me highlight what I take to be the three most crucial parts of the multipart answer to the question of how to handle complexity as a supra- and trans-scalar problematic.

First, one should not be stymied but persist in intellective work. More specifically, one should endeavor to make connections among things that are dually partial — connections pretending neither to be exactingly or exhaustively complete nor to emerge from a somehow simultaneously neutral and omniscient perspectival position — and, at the same time, to *know,* and to mark reflexively that one knows, that the connections one is making are thus partial. Drawing on the work of Donna Haraway, Strathern invokes the image of the "cyborg, half human, half machine," as an illustrative one through which to comprehend the embodied subjectivity of the scholar making these kinds of partial connections: an apt image because a cyborg, like

---

4   Ibid., xxiii.
5   Ibid., xxix.

the thoroughly relational being that Strathern otherwise calls a *dividual,* has the capacity to convey "the idea of a person capable of making connections while knowing that they are not completely subsumed within her or his experience of them" — and who "can then," and thereby, "be neither one nor a particle in a multiplicity of ones, neither sum nor fragment."[6] The nonetheless "rational knowledge" produced by this kind of subject "would not," as Strathern writes more summarily and straightforwardly, "pretend to disengagement; partiality is the position of being heard and making claims, the view from a body rather than the view from above" — that is, a view from a body that is itself viewable and, when viewed with appropriate sophistication, understood as possessed of inward and outward-oriented complexity: a body neither whole nor part of a whole but rather a self-differential node in a network, a non-singular "one" connected variously to other, likewise variously self-differential nodes in that network.

Second, making partial connections on this cyborgian model undoes any putative ease with which the connections could be called comparisons. By contrast, and because of a cognizance of the partiality with which any perspective would be provisionally centered, the partial connector displaces *comparability* — predicated on the simultaneous fictions of center and periphery, of subject and object — and reckons rather with the co-extensivity and thus the *compatibility* of things in relation:

> The cyborg supposes what it could be like to make connections without assumptions of comparability. Thus might one suppose a relation between anthropology and feminism: were each a realization or extension of the capacity of the other, the relations would be of neither equality nor encompassment. It would be prosthetic, as between a person and a tool. Compatibility without comparability: each extends the other, but only from the other's position. What the extensions yield are different capacities. In this view, there is no

---

6   Ibid., 27.

> subject-object relation between a person and a tool, only an
> expanded or realized capability.[7]

In other words, partial connections are both generous and generative. They do not presuppose that privilege or mastery will
be entailed by any conditional position, because that position
is recognized in its relation to another or to others. And, more
than recognized — because also "realized" in relation to another
or others — the position is endowed with a specific kind of multiplicity, the multiplied "capacity" or "capability" that could be
construed as making of the position a *composition*, a composite
and compositing form.

Third, if the compositions available for rendering by and as
partial connections are rich in potential capacity, one such potential capacity richly worth actualizing is the capacity to connect components *at different scales*. The "person" and the "tool,"
named in the passage from *Partial Connections* that I just quoted, would be a paradigmatic example of connected things that
are "not built to one another's scale"[8]; yet just because a "lack of
proportion" appears to obtain in this partial connection does
not mean that one should revert to the kind of thinking of, with,
and through wholes and parts that, as I have already suggested
in my gloss on the dividual or cyborgian body, is incompatible with the version of compatibility that Strathern advocates,
short-circuiting the logic of "parts and total systems":

> At first sight, a "tool" still suggests a possible encompassment
> by the maker and user who determines its use. Yet our theo-
> rists of culture already tell us that we perceive uses *through*
> the tools we have at our disposal. Organism and machine are
> not connected in a part/totality relationship, if the one can-
> not completely define [among other qualities, the complexity
> of] the other. Switching perspectives — as between anthro-
> pology and feminism — requires neither that a position left

---

7   Ibid., 38.
8   Ibid., 39.

behind is obliterated nor that it is subsumed. In turn, neither position offers an encompassing context or inclusive perspective. Rather, each exists as a localized, embodied vision.[9]

The work of "[s]witching perspectives" that Strathern explicitly conceptualizes and implicitly champions here is also, often a matter of *switching scales* — or, more nearly, of sliding scales, of slipping scales, and of determining, in any "localized, embodied" enactment of such sliding and slipping, the most sanguine relation between the two orientations to scale. Indeed, Strathern produces just such an enactment in this passage when she slides from one scale of conceptualization (at the level of discrete person and tool) to another, putatively more "encompassing" — but only *partially* more encompassing — one (at the level of abstract organism and machine); when she then slips to yet another scale of conceptualization (at the level of scholarly discipline, anthropology, and political discourse, feminism); and as she negotiates the connections among the sliding, the slippage, and the matter distributed across them by refusing either to "subsume[]" person and tool to the schema of organism and machine or to "obliterate[]" the anthropological person/tool or organism/machine dyad through a cyborg-feminist deconstruction thereof. Instead, she lets these rhetorical and argumentative moves stand in propinquity to each other, no one of them exactly "encompassing" or purporting to be "inclusive" of the rest as, alternatively, they extend out and toward each other in radiant reach, touching nearness.

Of course, this enactment of connecting partially and, in the process, of navigating scale is highly abstract and almost subterranean, beckoning for a way like mine of reading Strathern's way of thinking to draw out how it works. A more concrete demonstration of the method emerges later in the book, when Strathern elaborates an imaginatively associative yet also deeply informed meditation on the partial connections among Melanesian "men and trees and spirits and flutes and women and

---

9   Ibid., 40 (emphasis in original).

canoes." In her interpretive dance with these figures, Strathern argues that they "can all be seen as analogs of one another," if we attend with her to "[w]hat is being cut and being made to move" — including "imagery itself" — in the various and variable yet related practices in which (for instance) "people are cutting [a] tree out of [a] forest as an image of a man," or in which a "man dances with [an] effigy above his head" and "makes [a] combined image of tree and forest move between himself and the edifice he supports."[10] Yet just as important as this demonstration is Strathern's meta-critical meditation thereupon, which in glossing the demonstration provides an instruction for further work of this sort.

The instruction also figures as a rejection of the mode of obviational analysis championed by prominent anthropologists like Roy Wagner, for whom the notion of prefiguration is key to the interpretation of Melanesian myth and ritual. By contrast, and in highlighting the limits of obviational analysis, Strathern understands Melanesian dividuals not to depend on the predictability of chains or sequences of activity, in which one thing substitutes for another that prefigured it — and will be replaced by yet another that it prefigures — so that the world may be composed and recomposed reliably. Rather, she views Melanesian dividuals acting in such a way that their perpetual remaking of the world is also, paradoxically, its breaking down or *de*composition. As she puts it:

> I have indicated that there are some very fine analyses to hand in contemporary Melanesian studies [such as Wagner's]. We would be deceived, however, to think they afforded a self-sufficient dimension, as though they were simply completing the prefigured world which Melanesians take as their starting point. Melanesians use movement between persons to decompose their world[11]

---

10 Ibid., 112.
11 Ibid., 79.

As Strathern attends to them, we see that these decomposing movements have two further, crucial qualities: in their pulsations, expansions, contractions, and perspectival shifts, the work that they do is scalar; and in their borrowings from other paradigms, they provide a model for the Strathernian anthropology that in its turn borrows from said movements:

Communities expand and scatter again as, gathered in from their dispersed gardens, people become momentarily conscious both of their own centrality and of the necessity to maintain relations with other centers on their periphery — a contraction and expansion of focus. That contraction and expansion is mirrored in the way individual men decorate to expand themselves and then shrink to human size afterwards. [...] The view from the periphery is another view from the center, a version *composed* of the diverse named communities brought into communication with one another through men's efforts in ritual congregation and outward exchange. [...] What is at issue for these Western Lowlanders is the further possibility of making one's own interior out of the interiors of persons centered elsewhere, of "borrowing" culture.[12]

In this account, Melanesian borrowings of knowledge, predicated on movements that are themselves predicated on scalar shifts, enable the *composition* of partial, provisional views. And these views are at the same time *decompositions* of putatively settled worldviews (and of the likewise, putatively settled interiorities of beings, as well as of any centrality associated with those beings' positions). By extension, Strathern is not just partially connecting her own "conscious [...] contraction and expansion of focus" to the foci of her Melanesian counterparts, but also conceptualizing the very method of connecting partially as work requiring such reflexive scale management. In other words, Strathern is, like the "individual men [who] decorate to expand themselves," making a concrete move — connecting her

---

12 Ibid., 84–85 (emphasis added).

work to their practice to expand, likewise, her work's circumference — that also constitutes an abstract proposition (or, perhaps, preposition) about how to do such work. In the process, she arguably undoes, or decomposes, the very distinction between concretion and abstraction and transforms how we might weigh abstraction and concretion against each other (indeed, whether to weigh them thus, at all).

In one of the finest meta-critical readings of Strathern's own meta-critical maneuvers and provisions, Holbraad and Pedersen tease out one crucial effect of her transformation of abstraction as it relates to concretion: she gives us a way to identify scales that become things and things that scale themselves. Building on — and intensifying — this insight, they call Strathern's own intensification of abstraction an effort in *abstension:*

> Abstension is what happens to abstraction when the distinction between abstract and concrete itself is overcome, as it is in Strathern's postplural universe. Indeed, one way of characterizing abstensions would be to say that they are what abstractions become when they are no longer thought of as generalizations [...]. Rather, abstension is what happens to abstraction when it turns *intensive,* [...] and [...] refers to the way in which comparisons are able to transform *themselves* in particular ways.[13]

With a slight recalibration — and building on my prior thinking about the *ob-* prefix, as well as on Strathern's magnetic attraction to *ob-*prefixed words in *Partial Connections'*s salient passages in and on abstraction — I would rather call Strathern's version of abstraction a method of *obstension.* If "the prefix *ob-* may mark the paradoxical conjuncture of seemingly opposed meanings," if "an *ob-* position can be oriented both 'toward' and 'against' an object," and if "an *ob-* movement may obtain as a 'fall down' [...]

---

13 Martin Holbraad and Morten Axel Pedersen, "Planet M: The Intense Abstraction of Marilyn Strathern," *Anthropological Theory* 9, no. 4 (2009): 371–94, at 379.

or as a 'complet[ion] in intensification,'" then *obstension* may well name the kind of intensive, abstract intellection that works toward making connections, and thereby completing compositions, by also moving against them: by exposing their partiality through decompositions and fallings down.[14]

In the chapter of *Partial Connections* that I have been citing for its meditations on de/composition and (as) transformation, Strathern also moves recursively to the idea of the "remainder," a term that her foreword introduces, in thinking about questions and their answers, to designate "material that is left over, for it goes beyond the original answer to [a] question to encapsulate or subdivide that position (the question-and-answer set) by further questions requiring further answers. Or, we might say, it opens up fresh gaps in our understanding."[15] In revisiting the remainder in the context of conceptualizing what I call obstensive intellection, she adds: "One of my present purposes is to show the way anthropologists' activities constantly create 'remainders' for themselves, starting points for apparently new but not quite independent dimensions."[16] Indeed, *Partial Connections* itself creates just such remainders, of which I would highlight two as most intriguing: (1) what happens to scale as a concept — or, put another way, to *scale as scale* — in de/composing processes of obstensive intellection? And (2) what more may we learn about de/composition as such by also learning more precisely what it does to scale?

Strathern herself takes up these remainders in two seminal pieces from the 1990s, "The Relation" and "Environments Within." In the first, Strathern is once again theorizing connectivity, or what in this instance she calls the relation, about which she asserts that, on one view, the relation or connection is unaffected by scale. Moreover, she associates the relation with holography on the basis of the assertion that it is unaffected by scale; and in that relation or connection *of the relation itself* with

14 Nick Salvato, *Obstruction* (Durham: Duke University Press, 2016), 9.

15 Strathern, *Partial Connections*, xxii.

16 Ibid., 79.

holography, the relation produces scale-slippage (relations and holographs do not appear to belong to the same order or level). At the same time, and on another view, the relation is also associated with the irreducible complexity that (as we have seen before) exists as a constant across and despite scales. Yet in order to recognize such complexity across and despite scales requires *ipso facto* some recognition of scale — so that in the relation or connection *of the relation itself* to complexity, the relation produces scale-maintenance.[17] Working with and through these remainders from *Partial Connections* creates a further one, which we could aim to capture with the question: What exactly does the overlaying of scale-slippage and scale-maintenance produce? Logically, perhaps a paradox; affectively, perhaps ambivalence for scale; intellectively, perhaps cognitive dissonance about scale; and formally, I would argue — and argue that it is most important — Strathern presents a composition of scale in scale-maintenance that cannot be reckoned apart from, indeed that cannot be generated apart from, its decomposition in scale-slippage. In other words, at the level or scale of scale itself, de/composing practices of obstensive intellection corrugate and involute — and thereby intensify — their originary investment in de/composition.

Keep this intensification in mind as I pivot now to "Environments Within," where Strathern associates scale with the Western philosophical position that environments are outside humans and their activity (that is, their activity "on" those environments). By contrast, she associates analogy with the non-Western philosophical position that environments exist within beings. The first position is scale-sensitive, the second scale-insensitive; and an attendant irony — or, more plainly, insight — is that, ethically speaking, one may need to connect (partially, in both senses) the second position to the first in order to take proper responsibility for activity that is perceived to be "out there" in the world. Beings, Strathern posits, will care more

---

17 Marilyn Strathern, *The Relation: Issues in Complexity and Scale* (Cambridge: Prickly Pear Press, 1995), 5–32.

about and more fully appreciate the dimensions of their activity — and the likewise dimensional responsibility for that activity — if they understand outside environments, at least in part,
as also within.[18] Thus Strathern establishes a relation between
two positions that would seem to oppose each other; and, in
this case, the remainder also thereby established might be said
to obtain in the question: What happens to scale itself when a
scale-sensitive and a scale-insensitive philosophy are connected
partially to each other? To which we might answer, it neither
stays nor goes. Indeed we could say, from another perspective
on an issue already under exploration, that in this philosophical
conjuncture, scale is decomposed in such a way that we can still
apprehend the composition within the decomposition.

In so reading the two essays, I have been moving — partially — toward the notion that there is a relation between "The Relation" and "Environments Within." Both pieces could be said
to point toward the production of, and at the same time really
to be producing, scale's de/composition. But where the former
routes that de/composition through questions about fundamental acts of creativity and cognition undertaken by subjects like
Strathern, the latter adds dimension to the de/composition by
drawing a relation between (for instance) Strathernian acts of
creativity and cognition and (for instance) Melanesian acts of
creativity and cognition. That drawing of a relation establishes
a connection *between* two ostensibly separate things: a movement outward. Yet the second thing in the relation, Melanesian
perspective, demonstrates its own internally complex relational-
ity or connectivity. It is a thing with a relation *within* itself (the
recognition or emplacement of the environment *within* the being) — that is, a reflexive relation within itself *about within-ness*.
As she discloses as much, just as reflexively, in writing, Strathern uses an outward-oriented move (drawing her connection

---

18 Marilyn Strathern, "Environments Within: An Ethnographic Commen-
tary on Scale," in *Culture, Landscape, and the Environment: The Linacre
Lectures 1997,* eds. Kate Flint and Howard Morphy (Oxford: Oxford
University Press, 2000), 44–71.

between herself and others) to enable an inward-oriented move (describing the further connection within her connection's second element), which redoubles the movement inward constitutive of the second thing. In thus simultaneously amplifying and pressurizing the stakes of her lines of thinking, Strathern introduces a scale-maintaining extensiveness in the move from "The Relation" to "Environments Within" and a scale-slipping intensiveness in the move from "The Relation" to "Environments Within."

As we chart the movements partially connecting one of Strathern's writings to another and another, we would be mistaken if we took her to be constatively prefiguring and then refiguring a conclusion about scale — namely, that it is at once unusable and indispensable. Rather, she is performatively enacting and reenacting an abiding belief about scale, with different inflections, accents, and emphases (motivated changeably because the related concepts and phenomena with which she reckons alongside scale, like holography, complexity, and analogy, also change). And that abiding, organizing belief is that scale must be perpetually composed in, through, and as its own decomposition — and, better still, in ever more intensively spiraling, also extensively soaring, ways. Performing in this fashion connects Strathern (again, partially) to the Melanesians about whom, as she claims, we would likewise be mistaken if we were to take prefiguration as a cornerstone of their sociality. Near the end of *Partial Connections,* and in what she calls "a footnote to the concept of prefiguration," Strathern "adds" of the concept:

> In one sense, everything is in place: sociality, the values, relationships. But what must be constantly made and remade, invented afresh, are the forms in which such things are to appear. Potency has to appear as a new-born child or a bursting yam house, or a successful hunt, strength as shouldering a tall spirit-effigy, in the same way as social persons have to appear as members of this or that group. So those Melanesians who have origin stories, speak of heroes scattering the land *with the right form* in which tools or food or sexual attributes

or named groups should appear, just as the Gawan ances-
tress did. She did not have to show the men how to make a
canoe — that they knew — but in showing them the appropriate materials, she showed them the appropriate form it
should take.[19]

Turning to television with Strathern's lessons in mind and her
tools in the arsenal, one could compose and decompose television's scales again and again — and, on each recursive and intensive iteration of thus de/composing, one could do so with the
intention to match the changing form of the de/composition to
the likewise changing televisual concepts and phenomena that
one is arraying in constellation. For the remainder, as it were, of
this chapter, I will perform one localized version of such scalar
de/composition, in the case at hand taking the particular form
that it does because the de/composition entails an examination
of the key televisual phenomenon of miniaturization.

* * *

Perhaps readers are now poised to find it fitting that I begin the
next and final movement of this chapter with a turn to a striking appearance that Marilyn Strathern herself made in television in 2002. The occasion was the airing on U.K.'s Channel 4
of an episode of *In Your Face,* a series of eighteen ten-minute
films produced by the network, in which prominent Britons and
their portraitists share reflections about the portraiture with
documentarians Christopher Swayne and Bruno Wollheim.
In Strathern's case, as viewers learn through a series of cross
cuts from interview footage of her in her Cambridge office to
interview footage of her portraitist, Daphne Todd, in her studio, the portrait was commissioned by Girton College, where
Strathern was headmistress in the early 2000s, and it was meant
to join the series of portraits of all the prior headmistresses of

---

19 Strathern, *Partial Connections,* 98 (emphasis in original).

Fig. 1. Marilyn Strathern is partially connected to her dividual portrait. Source: Screen capture from *In Your Face.*

the college, dating back to its founding.[20] Wishing to establish a relation with Todd through which an unconventional artwork would be made — and thus arguably wishing also to preempt the determining process of prefiguration and refiguration through which the next installment in such a series of institutional portraits could be expected to participate — Strathern presented Todd with a piece of her own writing on portraits, which she had been invited to produce for a conference and which, in this event, seemed fortuitously poised to share as a gift with Todd. Yet if, following Strathern's own gift theory, the detachable part of oneself that one proffers can only be proffered as a gift when its recipient recognizes it properly, the paper was no gift, as Todd found its argument both wrongheaded and over her head: "My words failed," Strathern recounts. All the same, the putative failure figured as just one node in a network of con-

---

20 *In Your Face:* "Dame Marilyn Strathern (2001), by Daphne Todd," dir. Bruno Wollheim, Coluga Pictures for Channel 4 (original broadcast: 2002).

versation, posing, and painting that did, in the fullness of time, yield the effect of unorthodoxy that Strathern hoped the portrait would achieve: Todd found her way, during the course of Strathern's sitting, to representing Strathern as two-headed (and thereby dividual), both looking down as if to read and meeting the gaze of Todd, whose striking approach won the resultant work the Royal Society of Portrait Painters's Ondaatje Prize for Portraiture in 2001. Notably, in the television documentary, the dividualizing effect of making Strathern two-headed — literalizing by drawing out a relation of Strathern to herself, otherwise pulsing within herself — is recursively amplified and also intensified, as television frames a picture of Strathern sitting in her office beside the framed portrait that pictures her in that office (Figure 1). Simultaneously, an environment without, the exterior of Girton College represented in the painting in side panels, becomes an environment within the office once the painting is situated there for the duration of Strathern's interview.

Partial connections abound in the documentary, as well as in the embodied acts before and behind its making: of the commission to its precursors; of Todd's hands to her materials as she applies brush to birchwood; of Strathern materially to her office and symbolically to the institutional role that it emblematizes; and — most important — of Strathern and Todd to each other and to the painting, whose final incarnation, to re-cite language of Strathern's, takes "the right form" because of the ways in which the encounter of the sitting provoked recursions and reciprocities. In their turn, those recursions and reciprocities enabled Todd to innovate, generating and crossing what Strathern might call *cuts* (themselves mirrored in the cross cuts of the documentary). In the painting, and then redoubled in the documentary, one Strathern "exists cut out of or as an extension of another" (and another), at the same time that "these extensions — relationships and connections — are integrally part of the person" who is more singularly discernible as Strathern because "[t]hey are [Strathern's] circuit."[21] Or, to return to other

---

21 Strathern, *Partial Connections*, 118.

language adapted from Strathern and to connect it partially to the language of cutting and circuitry, I would add that Todd's composition comes to take what I have been calling "the right form" because, in the circuit of its making, composition itself is "remade, invented afresh" in the form of a *decomposition* of Strathern and her Cambridge world. Moreover, the decomposition testifies to the irreducible complexity, at every scale of Strathern's being and of her world, to which the painting — and then television — asks us to attend.

This analysis produces a remainder: the Strathern (and Strathernian) episode of *In Your Face* may be taken as a thing that scales itself, maintaining but also slipping scales in the service of animating the decomposition that also animates the making of the portrait. If so, then where may we locate an adjacent (or perhaps not-so-adjacent) scale that makes a thing of itself — to which to connect the episode, partially? One answer — the pop-music *mash-up* — suggested itself to me as the result of a dream that I had in a hotel in the course of writing this book (and after all, television, or at least television as partially represented by *The Sopranos,* instructs us to take seriously the strange connections between hotels and dreaming). In my dream, singer-songwriter Tori Amos shared with me a photograph of her embracing a woman whom she described as her mentor — and whom she named (and the photograph portrayed) as Marilyn Strathern. In a playfully associative way, the dream prompted my thinking about a remainder from my book *Obstruction* (more specifically, from the meditation therein on Amos's career), an object about which I did not write explicitly in the book but well could have: a live mash-up performance, recorded by a fan and posted to YouTube, in which Amos draws surprising — but once heard, unhearable — lyrical and musical connections between "Pictures of You," a hit for the band The Cure in the 1980s, and "The Big Picture," the opening track from her obversely, disastrously failed late-80s album, *Y Kant Tori Read.*[22]

---

22 Tori Amos, "Pictures of You/The Big Picture - Washington, D.C.," *YouTube,* August 16, 2014, https://youtu.be/XmGj25YO5NE.

To understand the mash-up as a self-thingifying scale is, or at least should be, fairly straightforward. Embarking on a mash-up means conceptualizing in a scalar way, measuring variously sized bits of lyrical and musical information in order to discover how, eventually, putting two songs into contact with each other — a thinging enactment of the scalar conceptualizing — may yield a pleasing aesthetic surplus. Similarly, to call the amateur video of "Pictures of You/The Big Picture" a species of television is, or at least should be, basically uncontroversial in our current media ecology. As we see in any number of directions in which we might turn, television, as a phenomenal and material field, capaciously arrogates many things to itself; because, for instance, the Apple TV connected to my living room's flat screen incorporates YouTube, I can watch "Pictures of You/The Big Picture" on exactly the same couch and in more or less precisely the same posture and position in which I watch *How to Get Away with Murder* as it airs in real time on ABC, *Project Runway* through my DVR, *Juana Inés* via Netflix, and on and on. Potentially more controversial, by contrast, is the eking of a partial connection between the Amos video and the Strathern documentary. (Wouldn't it be more sensible, say, to think about the documentary alongside contemporaneous Channel 4 programming, or the video in the context of similarly conditioned fan labor?) Yet I find value in the partially connecting move to the extent that observations may be made, propositions tested, and questions posed, that would not likely be glimpsed except through the eccentric partial connection.

Some of the questions begin as formal ones, then prosthetically extend their reach. When a fan records Amos drawing a partial connection between "Pictures of You" and "The Big Picture," to what extent is the resultant artifact — and its viewing — dividual? How many heads are brought together? Similarly, when Swayne and Wollheim film Todd, Strathern, and her portrait, to what extent are they performing a mash-up — and what things, potentially, are not only mashed in the sense of mixed but, in another meaning of the term, also *smashed* in the process? Reliably measurable size, as an instantiation of scale, may be one of them.

Fig. 2. Strathern's chair is haunted by her present absence. Source: Screen capture from *In Your Face*.

As the title of Amos's failed, then redeemed, song would have it, Todd's portrait of Strathern is a literally big picture, an aspect of its being that we would grasp readily if we saw it hanging in Girton College. Yet on the small screen, any available sense of the portrait's bigness diminishes precisely because of television's tendential function as an apparatus of diminution — or, more nearly, of miniaturization. Yet if the televisual version of miniaturization volatilizes scale, one upshot may be the invitation to enjoy scale-slippage and the complexity that it does *not* diminish if, in this case, we ask of and through the slippage: What is bigness, in the end? A level or grade (as in the place in the charts of The Cure's hit song)? A status (as in the respective prominences of Amos and Strathern in their professions)? A force (as in the norms and imperatives regarding, for instance, age and gender that both women have had to navigate, albeit quite differently)? A destination — or its voiding — or its generation as void? This last question emerges, partially, from my attention to what happens to "The Big Picture," a song about youthful career ambition and vanity, when it is reimagined by a fiftysomething

Amos in collision with "Pictures of You" — which is to say (once more, with Strathern), when it is "remade, invented afresh" on the other side of ageing through ambition's gradual loosening and through a reassessment of vanity, now viewed from a more autumnal perspective. In the process, the song transforms into a poignant reckoning with Amos's and her multiplied audiences' inevitable mortalities, the big unifying picture of death. Here, in other words, may we find another composition as decomposition, and the poignancy that I hear in it could be both amplified and intensified through one, last partial connection of the decomposed to the decomposed. In one room, a darkened auditorium, lyrics in Amos's mouth lose shape and form as she sings, "You finally found all your courage to let it all go, to let it all be, let it all, a—oo—ll, a—ooo—h"; in another, a brightly lit office is now empty of its holder, as a final documentary shot images an academic robe no longer possessed of the shape and form that the body would give it, a remainder hanging slack over the back of a chair — and Strathern gone into the cut (Figure 2).

2

Three Binarisms

In/On

My reckoning with the prepositions — which is also to say, propositions — *in* and *on*, both for television studies and for television as such, began in my mode as a grumpy grammarian. The grumpiness resulted from the staggering number of occasions and ways that I encountered all sorts of subjects using the word *on* — for instance, what happens "on" an episode of a series, or what happens "on" the series across episodes, or what happens more generally "on" television — when it would be much more apt and appropriate to speak or write of what happens *in* an installment, *in* a program, *in* the medium or field of television. The abiding force and hold of the set of "on" solecisms, while irritating, also became upon more sustained reflection an eminently fascinating phenomenon to me. (Flattering myself for my perceived cleverness, I thought for a while one could write an essay about the phenomenon called, "On 'On'" — yet that thought gave way to the recognition, as we shall see, that to theorize *on* without also theorizing *in* would render a less complete and compelling picture of their televisual uses and abuses.) In the span of that reflection, I considered the eminently plausible possibility that *on*'s movement across televisual discourse is an inheritance from radio, a medium whose signature phrases, such as, "On the air," move facilely and with suppleness into television's terrain. I also considered the closely connected, likewise plausible possibility that a much more suitable suite of uses of *on* than those I was cataloguing — namely, iterations or variations of the ubiquitous clause, "The television is on," to describe the very ubiquity of turning on, or leaving on, a television receiver — might centrally star, as it were, in a partial constellation: a star radiating influentially outward to touch, indeed to encourage the coming into being of, all those other, more annoying instances of *on*'s usage.

Yet even if radio sets the stage, as it were, for television's *on* habit, and even if agreeable uses of *on* in either radio or television or both provide a tacit alibi and justification for *on*'s more disagreeable uses, those explanatory frameworks do not explain, in a wholly saturating and satisfying way, the *on* problematic. After all, the word *in* is just as ready to hand as *on*, so why should a wide variety of subjects, even or especially when made aware of the possibility of tuning in to *in* and thus moving on from *on* (say, to take one very modest set of occasions, when I comment "on" my students' *on*-laden papers), persist in, default to, and incurably groove on *on*? I would submit that the fixture of, bordering on a fixation with, *on* in televisual discourse has become as lodged and stayed as sedimented as it is because it indexes, however inelegantly, some ongoing, unresolved trouble in our comprehension of television's ontology (recall that provocative element of Newcomb's opening salvo, "No one seems to know just what the medium is"). The trouble is also indexed — humorously and delightfully — in a sequence from a memorable episode of *I Love Lucy*, "Lucy Makes a TV Commercial," which, like the clause in the previous paragraph, I will nominate to take a role as the central star in the partial constellation of this chapter's section, *In/On*; the sequence is described in a keen and vivid way by Lori Landay, worth quoting at length, in her pocket monograph, *I Love Lucy*:

> Advertising, magazines, and television itself made the placement, style, and attitude toward the television set a topic of

discourse [in the 1950s]. It must have been profoundly strange to purchase a television set and suddenly have strange and distant places "in" your living room. For example, in a wonderful sequence from one of the best *I Love Lucy* episodes, "Lucy Makes a TV Commercial" (May 5, 1952, which culminates in her Vitameatavegamin drunken act), Lucy physically inserts herself into the television chassis to demonstrate to Ricky that she would be great on [sic] TV. The levels of television narratives and frames are multiple: Lucille Ball, star and spokesperson for Philip Morris cigarettes, acting the part of Lucy Ricardo, acting the part of a Philip Morris spokesperson inside a television in the Ricardo living room, which is on [sic] the television in the spectator's living room. Ball calls attention to the permeability of these boundaries between home and television when Lucy leans out of the television frame to pick up the cigarettes she has dropped. When Ricky enters and tries to "turn the channel," Lucy pushes his hand away from the knob. In this scene, Ricky and Lucy enact the myth, the fantasy, of the immediacy of television and make comedy out of the intersections of home and television.[1]

Wonderful an interpretation as Landay offers of this sequence, and agree as I do that two of the concepts explored therein are "the myth, the fantasy, of the immediacy of television" and "the permeability of the[] boundaries between home and television," I do nonetheless find that some of the sheer *strangeness* of the sequence — which retains its strange frisson all these decades later, as well as its freshness, even for viewers like me who have seen it countless times — slips from Landay's account. (Indeed, conspicuously missing from the account is one of the most curious and striking elements of the sequence: to toy with Lucy and stop her antics, Ricky re-plugs the receiver into the wall outlet; then the receiver begins sparking and emitting smoke, and Lucy jumps up and out of her posture inside the chassis

---

1   Lori Landay, *I Love Lucy* (Detroit: Wayne State University Press, 2010), 11–12.

Fig. 3. Lucy is nearly barbecued in the television chassis. Source: Screen capture from *I Love Lucy.*

in order to avoid, in her deliciously evocative phrasing, getting "barbecue[d]" [Figure 3]). To put further pressure both on the weird sequence and on Landay's gloss of it, I wonder what remains to be unpacked about the relationships — the partial connections — among

(1) Landay's pointed scare-quoting when she names the phenomenon of "suddenly hav[ing] strange and distant places" — as well, we might crucially add, as strange and distant, yet also familiarly near, *people* — "'in' your living room";

(2) her casual, two-time use of *on* in the way that I have marked with *sics*; and

(3) Lucy's theatrical demonstration of performing, literally, *in* the television receiver in order to prove her worthiness to circulate over the air, in the ether: that is, "on" television.

In the process of wondering in this tripartite way, I also propose emplotting the sequence, and the scholarship that it chases, as the first entry in a likewise tripartite, partial constellation, of which the other two, similarly complex items are the following:

(2) Users of Wikipedia have produced a partial — which, in this case, is to say errantly incomplete — list of Anglophone television series, past and present, whose titles begin either with the word *In* or with the word *On*.[2] Though some of the omissions are not surprising because they are television efforts more rarely seen and collectively recalled (for instance, PBS's queer documentary series *In the Life*, or HBO's early experiment in televising stand-up, *On Location*) than series like *In the Heat of the Night* and *In Treatment*, the list, whose non-marking as partial may misleadingly suggest that its picture is not so incomplete, does nonetheless have heuristic value in its indexing both of the greater likelihood of television personnel to think with and through, and therefore mark their products with, *in-* rather than *on*-oriented phrases, *and* of the greater likelihood of those *in*-marked products to live in collective memory and by extension "on" sites like and including Wikipedia.

(3) *Iron Chef: The Official Book,* which chronicles the global popularity and success of the Fuji Television-made, cooking-competition series *Iron Chef* through descriptions of dishes, recipes, and interviews with cast members, is also highly, winkingly attuned to the staggering scale of the series's abundance ("Some 893 foie gras, 54 sea breams, 827 Ise shrimp, 964 matsutake mushrooms, 4,593 eggs, 1,489 truffles, 4,651 grams of caviar, and 84 pieces of shark's fin were eaten, to mention just a few statistics").[3] The book is simultaneously

---

2   *Wikipedia,* s.vv. "List of Television Programs: I-J," and "List of Television Programs: O," https://en.wikipedia.org/.

3   Fuji Television Network, Inc., *Iron Chef: The Official Book,* trans. Kaoru Hoketsu (New York: Berkeley Books, 2004), xiii.

reflexive about the various ways, crossing scales, that spati-otemporal orientations of in-ness and on-ness may be valu-ably deployed to convey a sense of the series's often eccentric maneuvers: "All chefs are equal in the eyes of an ingredient"; "You'll get insight from the first person to say, 'Hey, wouldn't it be interesting if, let's say, a cabbage was placed on an el-evator-like platform and brought up on stage?'"; "What I had in mind when I advised the production staff was that we should use utensils and ingredients that could be found in every household"; "I said, 'Let's create a culinary program where the menu isn't decided on in advance.' The concept be-hind the program was to 'create a culinary program where the menu hasn't been decided on in an atmosphere like the Harrod's food emporium'"; "There were usually four judges on the *Iron Chef*. On the battlefield, you cook according to your style and belief. But there were times when you adjusted your dishes according to the judges"; "[S]ince the *Iron Chef*, I understand that there is more involved in a dish. […] So even if I am stuffed, I finish everything on my plate. I have gained much weight" — and so forth.[4]

* * *

Taken together, the elements of this partial constellation in-dicate that, in both production and reception, television may provoke the disorientations and reorientations — threatening sometimes to become the non-orientations, or, obversely, the overdetermined orientations — of the embodied subject in time and space. It does so in part, but only in part — and perhaps more strongly at its inception but all the same in an ongoing way as methods and mechanisms of transmission evolve — because a highly plural we, including some of television's makers along-side their audiences, do not understand precisely how those methods and mechanisms work. In part, as well, and supersed-ing the challenges of our fuzzy or faulty cognition of tele-tech-

---

4   Ibid., n.p., xvi, 56, 69, 104, 173.

nologies, television keeps "on" producing occasions for ambivalence, shading into anxiety, about fleshy, fleshly subjectivity as
such, which sticks us to (or unsticks us from) times and spaces,
and through whose embodying any cognition, fuzzy, faulty, and
otherwise, is inseparable. Moreover, this ambivalence is one for
which a number of vital *in*-formations for understanding tele-
technologies have been activated and circulated: will television's
in-corporation or *in-stallation* of subjects constitute their thriv-
ing presence, their foundering dislocation...neither...both?
And versions of this question acquire yet another potent dimension or flavor when in and on are uncertainly entangled with
one another. Whether recording *I Love Lucy* or *Iron Chef*, are
television's personnel on a soundstage or in a stadium? Is food
on a plate or in a dish, on the tongue or in the mouth? Is it true
that we are what we eat on, or in how we are eaten; and are we
eaten, beaten — or, more sanguinely, sweetened — when we are
rendered by pixels in two dimensions? (Lucy's joke about be-
coming barbecue doubles morbidly down on Ricky's prior quip
that her chassis routine is "third-dimension" television.)

Perhaps the abundant proliferation of *In* titles takes some
measure of the ambivalence attending modern and contemporary subjects' in-evitable engagements with television: for better
and worse, we are "in" it, if by *in it* we mean everything from *in
a fix* and *in a mess* to *in the pink, in hog heaven,* and beyond. Less
reliable is the possibility that television's subjects will be con-
sistently, stably "on": not in the solecistic sense that I have been
charting (though probably conjured, implicitly or suggestively,
thereby) but in the colloquial register in which we speak and
write of athletes — or chefs, or comics — being "on" their game,
"on" top of their performance, "on" it, just *on.* Even the most
iron of the iron chefs is not always "on." By contrast, a major part
of Lucille Ball's appeal in her role as Lucy Ricardo — another
fantasy, alongside the one of immediacy, that her performance
occasions — comes from our assurance that Ball will indeed
always be "on," even *and especially* when Ricardo is off, under,
or down. In the majority of episodes of *I Love Lucy,* physical
comedy results from Ricardo's failure to execute a "straight" role

successfully; thus a tension develops between Ricardo's incapacity to perform dramatically and Ball's genius for comic performance, as she plays Ricardo's "failures" so incredibly well. This tension, which ignites a spark of difference between the series's diegetic and non-diegetic registers, has a magnetic quality, generates charm, and stirs pleasure.

Of course, charm and pleasure are just one part of the composite picture in which we dwell, and on which we dwell, as we live (with) television. We abide *In the Dark* — but also *In Living Color*. We are *In Search of...*something whose discernibility is just beyond us — even as it can be taken as hiding *In Plain Sight*. Chasing it in the blue light of the thickening prime time, we think that thing grows as if *In the Night Garden,* yet we may find ourselves far from the garden's fecundity, caught in the arid heat, catching our breath *On the Rocks.* Living (with) television, we are in *The InBetween.* We are *The Inbetweeners.*

Flip/Flop

It would be willfully perverse *not* to invoke the HGTV series *Flip or Flop* (and the relentless tabloid coverage of the marital implosion and divorce of its stars) in the context of considering television's flip/flop binarism — but in order not to flop in the making salient of that invocation, let me first flip to four other items that, taken together with *Flip or Flop*, will form (and deform, and reform) this chapter section's partial constellation:

(1) Imagine tracing television animation's simultaneously genealogical, remediated, and remediating relationship to the flipbook — a set of partial connections that could flip historically from, say, 1956's *Felix on Television: A "Flip-It" Book* to today's *Naruto* flipbook videos, posted by fans online. Indeed, imagine, in the manner and mode of a Borgesian meta-storyteller, rendering the history in flipbook form, then making a video thereof. The imagining is this item.

(2) To constitute the next item, let's flip between two biographical anecdotes:

(A) In *Flip: The Inside Story of TV's First Black Superstar*, Kevin Cook tells the story of how, performing a *Julius Caesar* parody for military colleagues in the 1950s, comedian Flip — born Clerow — Wilson acquires his nickname, a story that Cook associates with Wilson's eventual television stardom:

> Dressed in a parachute toga, popping the wide, expressive eyes that would help make him a TV star, he joked about "chowing-eth downeth" and "goingeth to hecketh," finally working his way from "lend me your rears" to a proclamation about an ancient Roman fruit cup. "I come not to bury Caesar," he declared, "but to seize your wife's berry!"
>
> More cheers. [...] He bowed. He did a sidestep in his toga. An airman in the hooting crowd shouted, "He flippeth his lid!"
>
> And the nickname stuck. *Flip* Wilson.[5]

(B) Then, in a later part of the book, Cook titles a chapter, "Flip Flops," to convey in shorthand a sense of Wilson's early 1960s-era vacillations back and forth from clean to blue material; a flip-flopping between oppositional comedic strategies whose opposition is arguably deconstructed by the introduction of a third term — *black* material:

> Long ago an uncle had given young Clerow a joke book full of what Flip later called "old slave humor — *dis, dat, dem.* Terrible stuff." Thinking back to the book's tall tales of "darkies" and "tar babies" outsmarting tigers, white masters, lynch mobs, and "God Hisself," Flip now began seeing himself as part of a tradition that led from Reconstruction-era minstrel shows through vaudeville, the Chitlin' Circuit, and Amateur

---

5   Kevin Cook, *Flip: The Inside Story of TV's First Black Superstar* (New York: Viking, 2013), 32.

Night at the Apollo. He set out to retool his act, cutting anything too blue to play on TV, writing material that had less to do with what he thought was hip and more to do with what he thought was funny. In those weeks, he said, "I found my blackness."[6]

(3) In the 1980s Showtime series *Brothers,* notable both as a relatively early example of original premium-cable programming and for its relative earliness in television history as a sitcom featuring gay characters, a first-season episode that figures newly out Cliff as ambivalent, bordering on forlorn, about outness also enfolds a reference to *Family Feud.* Partially connecting this episode to the series's pilot (which pivots on the coming out) to constitute this item, I could describe the narrative, imagistic, and conceptual trajectory as one in which Cliff flips out of the closet — and his much older, conservative brothers flip out. Then he flops on the couch with *Family Feud* as his family tries not to feud and as he flips and flops about how to navigate his gayness and what to do with it (how, in a partial sense, to *televise* it).[7]

(4) The next item — my essay, "Early Late Style in *Roseanne's Nuts*" — will be a partially phantom or closeted object. I drafted a full version of the essay in spring 2016, then revised its conclusion after the American presidential election in fall 2016, then did not know how to revise it further after the green-lighting, production, and broadcast of the *Roseanne* revival in 2017, then abandoned it altogether after Roseanne Barr's firing by ABC executives in spring 2018. Unable to flip, or to wish to flip, the essay into a publishable form now that sustained attention to Barr's 2010s career feels ethically wrong to me, I am nonetheless interested in what I take to be ABC's cynical flip-flopping regarding Barr's tendency to make

---

6   Ibid., 81.

7   Stu Silver, "Lizards Ain't Snakes," *Brothers,* Showtime (original air date: August 23, 1984).

offensive public pronouncements (activity that preceded the racist tweet that occasioned her firing, though whose level of offensiveness did not, in my view, rise to the level of her deserving banishment from critical engagement prior to 2017). I also wish to flip from that network "scene" to a scene in *Roseanne* spinoff *The Conners*'s pilot, in which Dan Conner flips around uncomfortably in the bed now ghosted by Roseanne Conner — a scene that makes yet more complex a performance genealogy to which I drew attention in my now ghostly essay:

Hauntings abound in *Roseanne's Nuts* — as, for instance, when in the episode, "Life's a Snore," Barr, having undergone treatment for the intransigent sleep apnea that makes her snoring raucously unbearable and undoes boyfriend Johnny Argent's rest, comes to bed wearing a baroque mask hooked up to a CPAP machine and mock-performs bedtime sexiness with hand cocked on hip. The gesture, as well as the scenario of which it forms a key part, moves in untimely rhythm with the much-repeated figuring in *Roseanne* of the Conners at bedtime, engaged in playful conversation and robust touch that intertwine the romantic and erotic. In the leaner, more autumnal repurposing of this figuration for *Roseanne's Nuts,* eros and romance give way to a different, early-late performance of intimacy; here, affect swirls gently through a quiet, minimal hug and attaches to the simple, spare fact of Argent and Barr each having a side in a shared bed — and humor resides not in jokes attached to sexy physical antics but in a cut from the tenderly sketched bedtime scene to an installment-ending, confessional-couch clip in which Argent lets loose an "*Exorcist* sneeze."[8]

And now, at last, to flip back to my first item: The highly mediatized breakup of Christina and Tarek El Moussa could have

---

8   Sean Travis, "Life's a Snore," *Roseanne's Nuts,* Lifetime (original air date: July 20, 2011).

made a flop of the home-renovation series, *Flip or Flop,* that chronicles their efforts flipping houses in the Southern California real estate market. Instead, they and their collaborators have endeavored to flip a narrative of failure, and thus to sustain the ongoing profitability of the intertwined real estate and television businesses. That endeavor is framed, partially, as concession-cum-affirmation in the series's new opening-credit sequence: there we are told that the El Moussas may not have worked on or worked out their marriage, but they — and their series — will still work.[9]

* * *

Beginning with and including Felix the Cat, a number of the animated creatures bouncing and shuffling their way across the pages of my imaginary flipbook perform expressive behaviors that emerge in the American minstrel tradition and then evolve into and through both vaudeville theater and early film and television. Whether or not Wilson is mindful of the affiliation between his own expressive performances and those of Krazy Kat and Mickey Mouse, he is, as Cook makes clear, mindful of and deliberate about his borrowings from minstrelsy and vaudeville — borrowings that would, as Meghan Sutherland argues, enable Wilson and his collaborators on the enormously successful *Flip Wilson Show* to establish "a calculated ambivalence," flipping "between putting on a race-show and showing up racial-political injustice" as the project that "defines the program's aesthetic [...] fundamentally."[10] Yet just as Wilson is looking backward to performers like Bert Williams as he crafts his persona and techniques, so, too, is he a pioneering force in the world of standup comedy, which, in the post-WWII period, distinguishes itself from vaudeville formally and spatially (paradigmatically, in the comedy club that recognizes itself as

---

9   "Season 8 Premiere," *Flip or Flop,* HGTV (original air date: May 31, 2018).

10   Meghan Sutherland, *The Flip Wilson Show* (Detroit: Wayne State University Press, 2008), xviii.

an entity different from if adjacent to jazz clubs and night-clubs). That world, in which numerous comedians, like Wilson, clock their time and pay their dues with the hope of flipping from the landscape of the clubs to the remunerative terrain of mass media — and in which effort most of those would-be stars flop — has occasioned the rises (and sometimes falls) of television figures as variously celebrated and disgraced in the twenty-first century as Bill Cosby, Louis C.K., John Leguizamo, Jerry Seinfeld, and — yes — Roseanne Barr.

To achieve and sustain mainstream success is a delicate, eminently disruptable act. Flipping the switch between "putting on a race-show and showing up racial-political injustice" — a maneuver for which "flippeth" performance, colliding racy timeliness and lightly fashioned erudition, forms a precursor and grounding — may enable one to address a major, multiracial audience, at least some of whose members are racist. By contrast, "flipping one's lid" (as a rougher part of our discourse might describe Barr's mental illness) in the wee hours of the morning, with a tweet wholly unalloyed and unfunny in its racism, is likelier, at least in 2018, to cause network executives to flip out. And of course, at the other end of the political spectrum, comedy that is more aggressively antiracist and left-oriented than Wilson's has been just as likely, historically, to flop rather than to flip the consciousness of mainstream audiences (cf. *The Richard Pryor Show*), though recent successes like *Atlanta* may give us measured hope for such comedy's flourishing, even as we may be nervous about the precise nature of its reception among some white audiences.

Using the remote control to flip from ABC or FX to HGTV, we encounter acts like the El Moussas' in reality television that, if eminently disruptable, are much less delicately subject to such disruption. For a genre that feeds directly on shame, embarrassment, and their intrication, almost no amount of mordant humiliation cannot become grist for the reality mill — and this fact is just as true in the context of series premised on the execution of a craft, skill, or professional set of tasks, as it is in the franchises guided by soap operatic flourishes less tethered to the world of work or even to intimate domesticity (monikers like *Housewives* notwithstanding). Perhaps *Roseanne's Nuts* would not have flopped had it made good on its punning title and, however cruelly, mined emotional and cognitive instability for whatever "entertainment value" it is supposed to have, rather than approximating effects modeled in a more fully scripted way in *Roseanne*. Bizarrely enough, Barr's life with Argent and her children appeared too normal and normative to motor a reality sensation.

With the notion of norms in mind, we might profitably flip to subjects' capacity (or incapacity) for mind-melding with "America's" norm-affirming opinions and judgments, as captured in responses to survey questions: the feat that contestants are asked to perform in *Family Feud*. It is a series that, since the hiring of former standup comedian and sitcom star Steve Harvey as its latter-day host, joins, perhaps surprisingly, the genealogy of performance sites that also encompasses *The Flip Wilson Show, Roseanne,* et al. (With Harvey at the helm, and driven by his pointed and reflexively political banter with guests, the series, perhaps likewise surprising, says more in the 2010s about race — and more smartly — than we may expect the game show format to conduce.) It is also a series, however much predicated on what I have just dubbed, "norm-affirming," that holds the potential to do another, even obverse, form of cultural work. What effect might obtain when, in response to Dawson's or Combs's or Harvey's prompting, a rotating panel on *Family Feud*'s master board flips up and open — and the language it contains upends a norm? Or, to flip to another not-wholly-predictable element of the game's construction, what might happen when an unruly guest, perhaps visibly or audibly announcing oneself as nonnormative, refuses to play along with the mind-melding imperative and says something shocking, audacious, or just plain weird? The homonormativity and tele-chromonormativity of *Family Feud* sometimes, slyly opens on and up to the queer, or at least perverse, short-circuiting of the status quo; and, as in the case of *Brothers,* reflexively enclosing *Family Feud* in a sitcom scene with perversely intricate, norm-disrupting dialogue may signal as much for the viewer attuned — flipped, as it were — to this possibility.

Whether in *Brothers, Roseanne, Roseanne's Nuts, The Conners,* and many other cases besides, television is relentless in its meta-imaging of people watching television. And that project offers us just one sliver of the trans-medial and trans-scalar preoccupation with representing people — sometimes even nonhuman people — watching television (on the second page of *Felix on Television,* the cat, poised before the family set on which a vaudevillean magician is imaged, declares to his child companion, "I wish I could do tricks like that and be on television!"[11]). It is as though television, supported in the effort by the allied media in its orbit, and obsessed with tricks in general, is obsessively fixated in particular on displaying the consumption of its avatars — as if to reassure us through a comforting trick and treat that those avatars, so evidently phantasms shading into phantoms, are all the same and nonetheless real: another "calculated ambivalence."

Binge/Purge

Lest this chapter cause an unfortunate sense of queasiness, often induced by (the idea, the reality, or the conjunction of the idea and the reality of) bingeing on television — and typically associated with the putatively staggering volume of material consumed on a putatively foreshortened temporal scale — I flip back from *Flip/Flop*'s use of a five-part constellation to *In/On*'s use of a tripartite one. In this case, and in a development of the relationship of volume to scale conjured in the previous sentence, the three elements of the constellation will, in their respective forms, each test assumptions about volume and scale as (1) a note longer than we tend to imagine when we think of and with the idea of a "note"; (2) a durationally short television special that could nonetheless be construed as epic; and (3) a

---

11 Irwin Shapiro, *Felix on Television: "A Flip-It Book"* (New York: Wonder Books, 1956), n.p.

compact set of statistics deployed to describe an enormous television phenomenon.

(1) It is altogether too easy, with just a tap or two, to purge notes from our smartphones, so I was pleasantly surprised to discover, in the course of this book's writing, that I had retained one from several years ago, in which I recorded reflections right on the heels of bingeing the first season of *American Horror Story*, which offers a take on the classic trope of the haunted house where the living and dead coexist. Here is a very modestly redacted version of the note:

Binge viewing may be understood as an effort, at the level of reception, to thwart the feeling of seasonally rhythmic and regularized, temporal sociality that has long been identified with serialized narrative television. And that "thwarting" may now be a more or less weak, minor response to the larger, neoliberal ways in which such temporal sociality has itself been thwarted: attenuated or, more troubling, made unavailable for many contemporary subjects, even those to whom we attribute privilege, choice, and flexibility (the flexibility to be flexible is itself a kind of trap or cul-de-sac). As for what is happening at the level of production — where television's makers are increasingly, keenly aware of binge viewing as a phenomenon, and as one whose lineaments are differently marked at this historical moment than at earlier ones — those producers may do the old thing and hope it keeps working, either for bingers or for more "traditional" viewers (the former of whom are likely to find that the old dog does not do tricks that work anymore); create with a double vision and actively generate material that splits the difference and offers one way in for bingers and another, parallel, *simultaneous* one for punctual viewers; or risk zooming past the "traditional," punctual viewers by designing fare that more aggressively targets, confers recognition on, and indeed *values* the bingers as bingers. And those socialized temporality-thwarting (and thwarted) bingers? They may not be as done with old dogs as they wish, both because those dogs are still trotting before them (and messing with the bingers' speed) and because their very binges, quite apart from what they're bingeing on, are a measure of and testament to an impartial grieving, an imperfect mourning, for a version of being in time that, however phantasmatic or etiolated some of its earlier incarnations may have been, is now strongly taken to be cancelled even in its hallucinative and withered varieties.

Binge viewing the first season of *American Horror Story*, we may be more apt to notice narrative inconsistencies and narrative elements that are un(der)accounted for. (Why can Tate and Hayden roam to a park and bar, respectively, while all the other ghosts are confined to the house except on Halloween? Why is Maura the only ghost who ages, at least in the eyes of the women [dead and alive] who see her? Why, when Tate finally remembers his crimes, is the effect not more devastating for him?)

But, arguably more important, we may question bigger narrative shapes, structures, and stakes that we may likewise see differently when bingeing. (This series suggests, at least initially, that the account of evil as it dominates the house and its denizens will be epic in sweep and will say something, supra-psychic and beyond individuality, about the relationship of this epic evil to motherhood's mediations, especially of birth, death, and the porosity between the two. But then it falters on this promise and serves up instead discrete mothers with smaller wants and needs and finally more particularized relationships to evil. Disappointingly, it's not that the birth of a new child or children will have a seismic effect on the house and its energy — for all the inhabitants — but, much more simply, that some women demand some children. And where the backstory for one of those demands — Rose's — is concerned, its motivating impact on Tate is wholly underdeveloped. We would need to see more of these two characters together, and possibly more of them together sooner, to treat as plausible his murdering and raping on her behalf. And since she is a colossally bad mother, why, on the basis of one slender scene of their intimacy, should we suppose that he would, for years, invest in her as a good substitute for his own bad mother? Likewise — and to pivot back to the bigger picture — why should we let go of the expectation, which early episodes encouraged, that we could expect an ampler disquisition on evil and maternity [the birth of evil as such?] just because a psychic medium gets a late, badly written speech in which she tells us, in effect, "Pay no further attention to the real evil behind the devilish curtain"? It's not that these questions wouldn't or don't obtain for viewers who are not bingeing, but rather that our sense of how badly handled these issues are may become clearer, because intensified, when bingeing.)

In short, what we're seeing is a lack of a careful game plan, experimentation, and decision-making on the fly. Phenomenally, this in-fact routine combination of television qualities is one that we may accept better, or at least attend to differently, when our viewing experience isn't pressurized through temporal condensation or truncation — when its stretches and lapses and lags mirror (or, more precisely, feel more like they're mirroring) those to which the producers of such series are themselves subject. But alongside this phenomenal consideration, there's also a generic and historical one. The recent rise of the thirteen-episode season — and the concurrent, rising use of this season shape to tell more "closed" stories — poises us to want and even to expect different things from television (like premeditated beginnings, middles, and ends — and *not* necessarily so-called "novelistic" ones, just legible ones).

Certain other, specifically televisual effects, as noted by other critics, may seep out of the programming when subject to binge viewing. (We may not, for instance, feel the conjugation of the seasons so strongly when *American Horror Story*'s Halloween episode is not hitched to late October, or the season finale to Christmastime — or at least when the viewing of these episodes is not spaced out by several weeks, as Halloween and Christmas are.)

(2) This constellation's next item is the eleven-minute video, "Too Many Cooks," which Adult Swim originally aired at 4:00am during their insomniac bloc of fake infomercials and which has since enjoyed a vibrant and fecund, beyond-viral online afterlife.[12] Described as "a parody of the musical introductions for family shows like 'Eight Is Enough' or 'Just the Ten of Us' — with a repetitive theme song that plays on the aphorism that too many cooks can spoil the broth — before turning into a scene of bloody, murderous, cross-genre mayhem,"[13] or alternately as a "regurgitation of the viewing diet of a 12-year-old with a huge cable package in 1992 [...] that [...] turns into an ultra-grim rumination on the rotten core of most nostalgia,"[14] the video smashes through its own scale-smashing premise of parodic hyper-accretion (of actors with captioned names, of television references, of visual gags) to pose dark questions about the inescapable ubiquity of television.

(3) Finally, consider the Wikipedia page for the internationalization of *The Biggest Loser* as a franchise.[15] Despite once featuring a now-scrubbed, surprisingly and weirdly worded opening gambit (even for Wikipedia), which linked the weight-loss competition errantly to fantasy football, the page did then, and does now, proceed to enable a mostly accurate (say, weighed against the encyclopedizing of *In* and *On* titles) counting and accounting of the nearly three-dozen global adaptations of the series, the numbers of seasons of and win-

---

12 Casper Kelly, "Too Many Cooks," *Adult Swim* (original air date: October 28, 2014).

13 Ian Crouch, "Looking for Meaning in 'Too Many Cooks,'" *The New Yorker*, November 10, 2014, http://www.newyorker.com/culture/culture-desk/connect-many-cooks.

14 Todd VanDerWerff, "Why the Internet Is Obsessed with 'Too Many Cooks,'" *Vox*, November 11, 2014, http://www.vox.com/2014/11/11/7191255/too-many-cooks-explained-what-is.

15 *Wikipedia*, s.v. "The Biggest Loser," http://en.wikipedia.org/.

ning contestants performing in those adaptations, and cross-serial records ("Heaviest contestant," "Biggest weight loss").

* * *

Technically, it would be possible, if agonizingly boring (in both senses), to count all the pounds cumulatively purged across all *The Biggest Loser*s. Is a connected, volumetric impossibility — measuring all the tears extracted from both *Loser* participants and *Loser* viewers — a beautiful impossibility...or a cheap one? A harder question: are (any of) those millions upon millions of tears cathartic, and would *catharsis,* in this context, mean purgation, purification, a combination of purgation and purification, or something else besides? On the one hand, I have never believed — quite — that the kind of studied and storied melodrama manufactured again and again and again in *The Biggest Loser*s has afforded cathartic experiences to the subjects hailed by its melodramatic calls. On the other hand, the releases set in motion by sentimental identifications, however predicated on misrecognition, projection, narcissism, and the ruses of empathy, might somehow yield more slender value, more lean and angular meaning, than its weightiest detractors would concede. And of course the metaphorizing use of modifiers like *slender, lean, angular,* and *weightiest* are, to say the least, fraught on the occasion of their deployment to consider the literalized shedding of weight in *The Biggest Loser* and, as an array of journalistic exposés has indicated, the cruel tactics and strategies, serving an even crueler optimism, that animate those shedding processes and procedures.

Who binges *The Biggest Loser* — and how may she answer the foregoing questions and navigate the foregoing concerns differently from either the casual or punctually paced viewer of the series? But maybe this line of inquiry is just too much. Maybe we should (mostly...but all the same partially) purge *The Biggest Loser* from contemplation. Its horrors, and they are legion, are much more excruciating ones over which to linger than those of "Too Many Cooks" and *American Horror Story.* Indeed, the

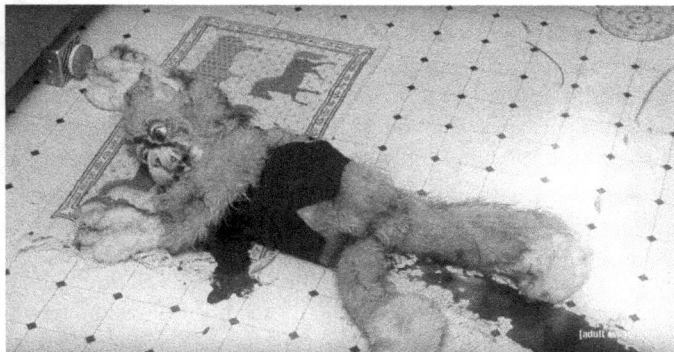

Fig. 4. Even intrepid SMARF cannot stop the onslaught of "Too Many Cooks." Source: Screen capture from "Too Many Cooks."

horror animating the latter two projects — just one dimension of a manifold and multipart excess in each effort — appears either in close proximity or even in the service of the sort of camp sensibility that never leavens *The Biggest Loser*'s melodrama. Yet the commingling of camp and horror does not quite unite the sensibilities driving *American Horror Story* and "Too Many Cooks," which could be said to perform obverse versions of generic and tonal hybridity: the former deploys camp in a maneuver to make tolerable, to cushion, the horrors that it accretes and hoards (and the series signals, even in its first season, that its makers crave to keep accreting and hoarding such horrors in an ambitiously ongoing instance of anthology — or it might be more accurate to say *repertory* — television); whereas the latter slowly bleeds out its camp, as it also literally purges the "characters" killed by a *Shining*-inspired madman, in order to produce a more devastating impact. As the video comes to its bleak conclusion, neither murderous mayhem nor the interventions of well-meaning scientists nor the attempt of a robotic cat named SMARF to detonate a bomb can stop the relentless onslaught of more and more "Cooks" (Figure 4). If camp is, as I have it, blood-let, then the bloodletting follows a logic — that of capital and its critique — in order to tell us something finally less Wildean than Beckettian about television: *This can't go on. It goes on.* And why, in the context of neoliberal global capitalism, should the lesson be otherwise? What force would halt the seemingly endless syndication of reruns, the proliferation of more and more and more DVD box sets, the repackaging of a successful brand for any and every national horizon?

Important as it is to train a critical eye on such futural prospects, looking critically backward forms a necessary complement to that work — and when we look thus, we will find that at least some of us have for quite some time been bingeing, albeit in different ways and registers and through different techniques from the ones now available. Indeed, why use the language of "regurgitation" and "viewing diet" to describe the "12-year-old with a huge cable package in 1992" except to cast him retrospectively as a binger, imagined as glued to the screen for hours and hours on end in order to watch new episodes of *Full House,* old episodes of *Family Ties,* and plenty of other banal fare besides? Perhaps along with his cable package, the tween had a VCR with which to record and save favorite programming that could also be binged for multiple hours at a stretch.

Whether we conceive of the binger then, now, or later, I do want to cleave from the rhetoric of bingeing the discourse of addiction that is altogether too likely, rather, to cleave to it. And I want to do so despite the brilliant ways in which, by contrast, Hunter Hargraves — quite aware of the ideological risks at stake — deploys addiction discourse to illuminate our understanding of contemporary reality television:

> Models of the mass cultural consumer as addict have circulated since the rise of commodity culture, and these have typically figured the addict in quite problematic terms of gender, race, and class. Yet while such discourses demand a critique, this does not mean that the notion of *addictive spectatorship* should simply be flushed down the drain like a bad drug. Indeed, one might deploy this model precisely to open up questions about bad subjects and objects. [...] First, I consider the representation of addiction on reality television through

a subgenre I call recovery television, in which the spectacular behavior of compulsive or addicted individuals must be diagnosed by experts and corrected through an intervention. [...] Second, I position the addicted spectator as a necessary counterpoint to the mechanisms of neoliberal citizenship inherent to reality television. Asking that scholars of television and popular culture take seriously television's drug-like properties, I show how these properties have become a critical mechanism of neoliberal culture's pathologizing of cultural affect. Taken together, these twinned assertions transform the once-iconographic figure of the television spectator — the (supposedly) sedentary, lethargic couch potato — into the hyperactive, amped-up TV junkie who gets high from multiple and often duplicated media platforms.[16]

Appreciative of the nuance and sophistication with which Hargraves constructs his model of addictive spectatorship, I wonder what "cultural affect" or affects — obtaining at what scales or their slippage — cannot be adequately described and interpreted either through the metaphorizing language of the junkie or the counterpoised language of the couch potato. If spectators are neither "amped-up" nor "lethargic," but, eking a third way, performing calmly attentive and critically charged viewing for long periods of time, perhaps they are better nominated as cook-mates, and perhaps we will not deem their broth spoiled.

---

16 Hunter Hargraves, "(TV) Junkies in Need of an Intervention: On Addictive Spectatorship and Recovery Television," *Camera Obscura* 30, no. 1 (2015): 71–99, at 72–73.

3

Five Keywords

Whereas each section of the prior chapter housed its own partial constellation, the five sections of this chapter are meant, themselves, to configure the stars of a five-part constellation — in order (among other effects) to recalibrate our sense of "the chapter" as a formal container, one that has a different scalar inflection. Redoubling that conceptual move, each section also focuses on a respective object that has a different scalar inflection from the other four main objects of the chapter. Working with a remainder from the final section of the prior chapter, regarding embodied consumption (or its refusal), *Weight* addresses a suite of performers in a range of programming focused variously on health, fitness, diet, cooking, or baking. *Rule* looks closely at a variety of interlocking audiovisual elements in just two installments of a proto-reality series, *This Old House. Map* homes in on a single graphic design element used in the reality television series *House Hunters International. Interval* engages a massive fan labor to transcribe the scripts of American daytime serials (and perversely mines a scholarly search tool designed to extract value from the resultant corpus) in order to identify the variable intervals that can be used for charting twenty-first-century language uses in said serials — and then to deform and reform the scales of those intervals. And, finally, *Ladder,* also furnishing a remainder about cults for the next chapter, traces in Hulu's *The Path* a tension between an overarching serialized narrative and a likewise overarching mythos about ladder-scaling, which obtains over the course of the series's run. Though it would give too much weight, as it were, to the keyword *ladder,* as opposed to *weight, map,* and the like, for me to metaphorize each chapter section as a ladder's rung (and, in the process, to suggest — misleadingly — a teleological trajectory from one section to the next), I do offer these progressive sections in their particular order with the invitation for you to read, across the cuts between them, a building intensification and a spiraling involution that depends in part on the sections' ordering and that ordering's way of connecting the sections partially to one another.

Weight

If the specters of addiction discourse and addiction spectatorship hang over this chapter as two of the Strathernian remainders from the prior one, then Jack LaLanne arrives just in time to offer a hangover cure. As he says in a paradigmatic, early 1960s-era installment of *The Jack LaLanne Show* — one of the easiest to hand because of its sharing on YouTube and its algorithmic rise to the top of a Google search — "What do I see? I see a lot of new students. And I see that these students are suffering from hangovers. Tsk, tsk, tsk. I guess you had kind of a rough weekend. I'm gonna show you what to do about that hangover! Get up on your feet, give me a big smile."[1] Amusing as it is to watch LaLanne proceed, punning, to clarify that he actually has the cure not for over-intoxication but for the flabby flesh "hanging over" here and "hanging over" there, resultant from poor diet and lack of exercise, I am less interested in him for his fitness philosophy and its manifestation in embodied techniques — or even in *The Jack LaLanne Show* for its massive scale as the longest-running exercise program in American tel-

---

1   jacklalanneofficial, "The *Jack LaLanne* Full episode (Hangovers)," *YouTube,* January 17, 2016, https://youtu.be/tP4oRWwhoRw.

evision — than for the partial connection that prominent scholars (and others) have made between LaLanne and one of his
storied television contemporaries, Julia Child. In a book focused
on Child's likewise long-running series, *The French Chef,* Dana
Polan asserts that "[w]hile Julia Child needs to be situated in a
history of *cuisine* in America, she also belongs to a history of
television and, in particular, to that common brand of nonfic-
tional hosted programs popular in the 1950s through the 1960s
and peopled by names such as Jack LaLanne, Zacherly, Officer
Joe Bolton, Vampira, and so on."[2] Similarly, Laurie Ouellette
links the two figures and, moreover, links them as exceptional
in a period "when lifestyle experts may have achieved notoriety
but were not treated as celebrities" and did not tend to "build
their own brands around their TV personas"; by contrast, "especially charismatic figures like Jack LaLanne, of the exercise program *The Jack LaLanne Show* (1951–1985), and Julia Child, host
of *The French Chef,* achieved […] fame and engaged in book
publishing."[3] Even a casual blogger with no evident expertise in
television history makes the partial connection when she writes
summarily, "Julia Child taught us to cook by way of the TV, and
Jack LaLanne taught us to exercise to keep the excess weight in
bounds also by watching TV. Each of them appeared on morning
TV for a half hour, and we learned how to make an omelet, and
how to do deep squats afterward."[4] Though the topics respectively highlighted here — of period-specific television trends, of
charisma's relationship to branding, of the obversion of exces-
sive consumption to athletic fortification or repair — are worthy
of the exploration they receive, how else might we weigh the
televisuality of Child and LaLanne with and against each other,
and with what upshots for comprehending television scales?

---

2   Dana Polan, *Julia Child's* The French Chef (Durham: Duke University
    Press, 2011), 12.

3   Laurie Ouellette, *Lifestyle TV* (New York: Routledge, 2016), 41.

4   Kayti Sweetland Rasmussen, "Father of Fitness," *Pachofa-Unfinished*
    (blog), March 7, 2015, http://pachofaunfinished.wordpress.com/2015/03/07/
    father-of-fitness/.

An answer may begin to emerge from partially connecting the episode of LaLanne's program cited above to the second episode of *The French Chef,* which comes to attention, among other reasons, for heading an *A.V. Club* list of ten representative installments of Child's series.[5] In these respective episodes, both LaLanne and Child use a discourse of *weight* to talk about their enterprises; and, not merely incidental or coincidental, when speaking of weight, both LaLanne and Child are speaking in the same breath about — and demonstrating the use of — simple tools (his hand on the back of his sole prop, a chair, her hand clasping a fine chef's knife). For his part, LaLanne tells the home audience that even the "girls" who do not have a "weight problem" may wish to "shrink" a "hanging midsection" — which requires an exercise in "contract[ion]" that he models, using the chair for support. For hers, and enthusing about a wedge-shaped knife with an eleven-inch-long blade, Child shares that she likes it because it is "so heavy" that it "does most of the work for you" as you chop (for instance) pounds of onions. Then she proceeds to share a knife-sharpening demonstration and embroiders her earlier enthusiasm for the knife's weight; when the knife is well-sharpened, having "take[n] the edge," it can be laid, Child says, on a tomato, and "just the weight of the knife would cut through the tomato." Better and more provocative yet, "if you laid it on your hand, and just drew it across, the weight would cut your hand right down to the bone."[6]

LaLanne and Child address their viewers in evidently different yet all the same related ways: both call attention to the changeability of the body, whether through sanguine fitness or grisly accident (and, likewise attuned to a version of fitness — for a task — Child later says that, with practice, one can chop onions very fast and not be likely to nick one's thumb). As

5   Robert David Sullivan, "Enjoy the Sensual Delights of Cooking with 10 Episodes of Julia Child's *The French Chef,*" *The AV Club,* November 21, 2012, http://tv.avclub.com/enjoy-the-sensual-delights-of-cooking-with-10-episodes-1798234736.

6   "French Onion Soup," *The French Chef,* PBS (original air date: February 9, 1963).

they do so in moments that call attention to the sensuous contact of their hands to chair and knife, they may also recall for us language of Strathern's, quoted earlier and worth quoting (partially) again, regarding the person-tool dyad: "At first sight, a 'tool' still suggests a possible encompassment by the maker and user who determines its use. Yet our theorists of culture already tell us that we perceive uses *through* the tools we have at our disposal. Organism and machine are not connected in a part/totality relationship, if the one cannot completely define the other."[7] Weighted, as it were, with their different meanings and histories, and belonging clearly to different scales of being, LaLanne and the chair, on the one hand, and Child and the knife, on the other, enter into a dance with one another. The dance's typical outcomes, however likely, cannot be determined or defined in advance by the human choreographers, to whom the tools become tantalizingly uncertain co-choreographers (though not as cheekily gruesome as Child, chair-using LaLanne does concede that one could misexecute a move, strain oneself, or fall during a fitness routine). At a small scale, then, these performers and their tools disclose something about "[o]rganism and machine [...] connected in a [...] relationship" that is applicable to myriad subjects engaged, as they are, with another machinic tool — television itself — whose co-creative motions with those subjects are properly understood as unpredictable, when examined in and for their complexity.

* * *

I cannot make a now-recognizable cut, signaled by asterisks, without in this instance thinking both of the onions upon onions cut by Child *and* of the signature crew-cut of Susan Powter, who catapulted to fame and, briefly, to fortune in the 1990s following the unpredictable, indeed runaway success of her 1993 infomercial *Stop the Insanity* and the various forms of merchan-

---

7   Marilyn Strathern, *Partial Connections,* updated edn. (New York: AltaMira Press, 2004), 40.

dise that it enabled Powter and her collaborators to hawk. Positioning herself as an opponent of the diet and fitness industries to which she herself could be said to belong, Powter, who doubled in size after a painful divorce but appears thin and toned in her infomercial — and for whom, "Forget your scale!" is a mantra (her calipers will tell you the truth and set you free) — rails in particular against the sellers of specialized diet foods. Their own mantra — or, more nearly, their barely subtextual cue, in figuring out whole meals for their clients — is, Powter says, "Don't think!"[8] The moment in which Powter observes as much is perhaps the most meta-televisual of her infomercial. Television is like the diet industry in its manifold invitations to non-thinking and unthinking, yet also like this local moment, television more globally enfolds, in some of its efforts and appeals, an asking of us for our (re)thinking of the unthinking or non-thinking.

And yet, in a further turn of the screw, Powter herself emerges over the course of the half-hour video as a would-be, cultish guru (hence my invocation of the word *mantra* to describe both Powter's language and the strategies of those whom she detracts). Like most gurus, she has a malignantly narcissistic belief in the power of her message, which she frames as the "most important [...] on earth"; and also like most gurus thus messaging, what she has to share is a cliché stunning in its banality: "You gotta eat, you gotta breathe, you gotta move." But the banality hardly matters, because what Powter is essentially selling — before, behind, and beyond her message or her branded products — is what Ouellette would call her charisma. It is a charisma predicated on frenetic, even frenzied, displays of energetic enthusiasm, as well as on joke-cracking that one might expect to find sooner in a standup routine than in a "lifestyle"-oriented infomercial; it is, moreover, a charisma that would be wildly off-putting to many, as the myriad, often savage, parodies of Powter's self-fashioning and self-presentation attest (though ever a cunning marketer, Powter is happy to get in front of the

---

8   Susan Powter, "Stop the Insanity," USA NETWORK for syndication (original broadcast: 1993).

potential for takedown by embracing *self*-parodies gentler than those of her haters — say, in the form of her appearance in the pilot episode of *Space Ghost Coast to Coast,* which provides a perfect métier for acknowledging and celebrating her goofiness and eccentricities[9]). As Powter cautions her audience against food weighted with fat, to which she contrasts high-volume eating of low-fat foods, she seeks, and succeeds in seeking, to wield her charisma to do a business likewise high-volume in scale, unweighted at last with rich meaning — but all the same saleable.

* * *

In a blog post for BBC *Good Food* titled, "Mary Berry's Top 10 Baking Tips," Berry's very first tip concerns the measured weights of a baker's ingredients: "1. Weigh the ingredients carefully. You wouldn't believe how much can go wrong just because ingredients have been weighed incorrectly. If you're just a little bit out it can have a catastrophic effect on flavour and consistency, yet it's one of the easiest things to get right. Just concentrate at the start because any errors will only be amplified going forward!"[10] What if one were to apply Berry's advice to *The Great British Bake Off,* the globally popular and enormously successful series in which she appeared as a judge of Britain's amateur bakers from 2010 to 2016? Given the substantial overhaul of various elements of the series between its initial six-episode season and its next ten-episode season — taking the form, in that second season, into which the series would settle for its ongoing run — most viewers would likely be inclined to say that the "ingredients [were] weighed incorrectly […] at the start." Indeed, Netflix executives wish so fully to distance the franchise from its origins that they have branded one of their 2018 offerings *The Great British Baking Show: The Beginnings* — and then begin

9   Matthew Maiellaro, Andy Merrill, Khaki Jones, and Keith Crofford, "Spanish Translation," *Space Ghost Coast to Coast,* Cartoon Network (original air date: April 15, 1994).

10   Mary Berry, "Mary Berry's Top 10 Baking Tips," BBC *Good Food,* http://www.bbcgoodfood.com/howto/guide/mary-berrys-top-10-baking-tips.

that set of episodes with the second season, recast on the Netflix site as the first. All the same, viewers can find easy routes, if less legal than watching via Netflix, to see those first six episodes, in which ten rather than twelve bakers "battle it out in locations across the country" (rather than in one setting, the storied bakers' tent of the rest of the series), as the never-imaged male narrator — gone by the second season — tells us in voiceover early in the pilot.[11] Also expunged from future seasons are interviews conducted by host Sue Perkins (or by Perkins with co-host Mel Giedroyc), which feature talking heads discussing the histories and evolutions of different baked goods. Coincidentally enough, a more constant factor in the packaging of the bake off and tied-in efforts is Berry's advice about weighing ingredients — a version of which, very near, rhetorically, to the writing for the blog, is sounded as the first language that we hear from her in the series's pilot.

Yet Berry herself would probably not wish for us to engage in this thought experiment and apply, across scale and form, advice about baking to the televised baking competition and thereby find the first season wanting. (After all, her look, much more glamorous in the second season and beyond, is one of the ingredients we would be weighing.) Indeed, the advice that immediately follows tip one in her blog post is to "[t]ake the recipe as a pretty full guide, but not an absolute blueprint." She elaborates:

> Sure, in terms of measuring out ingredients it should be uniform, but the way you knead cake dough, the instruments you use and particularly the strength of your oven will all have slightly differing effects on what you make. With that in mind, make your own comments on recipes so that you'll know for next time how your process and equipment affects the final product.

---

11 "Cakes," *The Great British Bake Off*, BBC Two (original air date: August 17, 2010).

Here Berry captures well what a Strathernian interpreter might call the irreducible complexity of each baking occasion — as well, we could add, of each recording and broadcast of the baking occasions that populate Berry's most famous series. Tracking that complexity effortfully would likely be at odds with a version of criticism as weighing, although composing the hypothetical game of criticism as weighing is a necessary step in its decomposition.

When the makers of *The Great British Bake Off* moved, chasing a more lucrative deal, from BBC to Channel 4 for the series's eighth and subsequent seasons, Berry, about as beloved a television personality as one may imagine, declined to make the departure with them, a decision touted as manifesting her loyalty to the BBC. And steadfastness is indeed an element of the complex recipe through which her charisma, enabling her abundant success across forms and platforms, renders Berry a delight to her devotees. Some of them will no doubt boycott the Berry-less *Bake Off,* in a would-be mirroring of Berry's perceived steadfastness. But loyalty has no place in the *Bake Off's* own complex recipe (though it has, in its eighth season, made room once more for talking heads on such topics as pudding), a recipe that appears to be working quite well for Channel 4 and Netflix — and that will likely continue to do so at other, coming forms and scales of distribution.

Rule

Making partial connections through the rubric of the first of five keywords, weight, also enabled the unfolding of five key concepts: brand, charisma, salespersonship, complexity across maintained scales, and connectivity of beings across slipped scales. All of these television elements could be identified, too, as inputs and outputs of *This Old House,* a program featuring serialized house renovation projects that has been airing on PBS since 1979 and that is probably likeliest to conjure, for television's memorialists, episodes from the 1980s portion of the series's run, when Bob Vila served as its host.

Absent a paid subscription to the streaming services featured on *This Old House*'s website, one may not alight reliably on episodes of the series featuring Vila or his immediate successor as host, Steve Thomas. My own viewership of episodes from 1991, most of them showcasing part of Thomas's and collaborators' work on a project called, "The Wayland House," was undertaken in a screening room at UCLA's Film and Television Archive. I chose to view these episodes mostly for their free availability during a trip to the archive, motivated chiefly by other investigations but allowing this partial addition; in the end, I was glad that the episodes, as it were, chose me and that one of them in particular, partially connected to others, disclosed to me how to begin to compose (and decompose) a criticism of (mis)rule.

Working with a remainder from the prior section on *Weight,* I am put back in mind, in the context of thinking about *This Old House,* of *The A.V. Club*'s thoughtful survey of *The French Chef.* That piece underlines how vividly Child's series images, again and again, close shots of her hands as she toils in her kitchen — and I would, now, connect that observation to ones I made in real time in the archive as I watched *This Old House*; for that series is likewise relentless in its close-ups of hands, using a variety of instruments and materials in the laborious course of houses' careful and caring renovations. Of the numerous such configurations and reconfigurations of the person/tool dyad that I noted while watching — in the process, configuring my own person/tool dyad with computer's keyboard — I was struck most by one that opens an episode in which master carpenter Norm Abram is about to outfit a bathroom floor with vinyl tiles while Steve Thomas observes the process. As Abram explains that he wants to "fill the voids" created by knots in the wood before tiling, he strokes such a knot with his fingers and thumb, and the camera pushes in to image the motion closely for us; in this moment, he is connected, knotted, to the knot. Then, when he proceeds to enlist Thomas's help and Thomas uses a tape measure — and follows Abram's charge to be very precise — they (and we) enjoy this dialogic exchange: Thomas: "Boy, you're really being fussy with those measurements, Norm." Abram:

"Well, you have to be, Steve. [...] If the room is out of square, you're gonna start angling off."[12]

Taking a cue from this scene makes me wonder how to perform a television criticism that recognizes the value of the square yet also takes the risk of "angling off," of letting the work go "out of square" — which could mean, among other effects, and as E. Patrick Johnson might have it, putting the *quare* back in *square* (or drawing the *quare* out of *square*).[13] How to square with series like and including *This Old House* and also to share what is quare or queer in one's experience of such series — and to avow, reflexively, that the latter aim is itself a queer one when the quare reading of a series is an acknowledged "misreading"? This challenge came for me vividly into view, as it were, when I watched the episode of *This Old House* in which Thomas visits the Society for the Preservation of New England Antiquities' Conservation Center in Waltham, Massachusetts. The journey from Wayland to nearby Waltham is undertaken for a consultation with the center's staff of conservationists, whose signal charge is the preservation of buildings on their site in Waltham but who consult ad hoc on other projects, like the restoration of the 1815 "Kirkland" house in Wayland showcased in the thirteenth season of *This Old House*. Yet before any of this information about the center or its personnel is plainly revealed, the teaser for the episode aims to draw us in more enigmatically and elliptically. Its close-up images yet another hand, this one pointing to an arrow on a television-like screen on which Thomas, an as-yet-unidentified man — and we — get a weirdly mediated view of some object (we won't yet discern that it is a very small extract from a window shutter); then the camera dissolves to a more recognizable window installation.[14] That dissolve suggests the close cor-

---

12 "The New Orleans House," *This Old House,* PBS (original air date: February 1, 1991).

13 E. Patrick Johnson, "'Quare' Studies, or, (Almost) Everything I Know about Queer Studies I Learned from My Grandmother," *Text and Performance Quarterly* 21, no. 1 (2001): 1–25.

14 "The Wayland House," *This Old House,* PBS (original air date: November 30, 1991).

respondence or connection between window and screen, as conceptualized by media theorists like Anne Friedberg.[15] It may also invite us to slip registers and scales, as the dissolve itself does, in our engagement with the episode and the series.

If we do, one especially slippery leap we may take is to read queerly the presence of the second man, architectural conservator Greg Clancey, as we meet him more fully in his paint-splattered apron — and as we see him also as tie-wearing, lisping, and gentle in his demeanor. When I watched the walk-and-talk scene in which Clancey tells Thomas about the center's work, I noted, "Clancey seems *super-gay*. It is taking this level of stealth gayness popping up onscreen for me to maintain interest in hour three of watching and taking notes on *This Old House*." Was it my confinement to the beige screening room at UCLA, where the couch was just a little too comfortably plush and the oxygen deprivation just a little too mounting, that induced my minor fever dream of *This Old Gay*? And was the dream especially feverish — or was there actually something *more* plausible in my queer account — as the episode continued to unfold and when I proceeded to type the following note: "More hand close-ups! After Steve's hand nearly touches Greg's as the latter holds an old molding across the edge of which Steve runs his fingers, Steve says, 'I'll come to you next time I need a molding' (!!!)." Reading for and through innuendo, euphemism, and allied forms of coded language is — justly — a cornerstone of queer theoretical practice. Yet having engaged in that practice for a long time, I ought to know how to *measure* when the practice is paradoxically "aslant enough" to yield a genuine and generative insight, when *so* aslant that the putative insight is off the mark. In this instance, I would not wish to defend my notetaking against the charge that it constituted a form of the latter errancy. I do, however, share the anecdote nonetheless because meditating on it — and because meditating further on *This Old House* as well — helps me to appreciate that, with time and space enough

---

15   See Anne Friedberg, *The Virtual Window: From Alberti to Microsoft* (Cambridge: MIT Press, 2006).

to scale my viewing experience otherwise, watching more and more of the series, I *would*, I will warrant, encounter moments in which the slender, delicate erotics of men's shared labor are indeed obtaining as a homoerotics worthy of such a nomination.

When at long last we get a clarification of what the teaser imaged, we learn that Thomas has come to the center chiefly to share paint samples taken from the Kirkland house in Wayland. Thomas hopes that, when the samples are subject to scrutiny under a special microscope kept in a "clean environment" in old service quarters at the center's main house, he, Clancey, and another conservator, Brian Powell (my notes call him, "another super-gay"), will be able to tell accurately what respective colors adorned the house's exterior elements in 1888. The men embed the samples in epoxy ice cubes; when they are popped out, they are ground down with a wet sander and made into cross-sections to investigate under the microscope. When we get that view with the men, the teaser's tease comes, as it were, into focus. One of the samples is under the microscope, and the attached monitor shows us cross sections, layers of paint and dirt particles from different periods. The arrow points to the key, late-nineteenth-century layer. Once more, a passage from my notes: "If you didn't know what you were looking at, you might think what's imaged onscreen in blue, green, and black is an extreme close-up of the inside of a small aquarium — or an extremely blurry distant view of a landscape with trees and flowing water." Something less willfully perverse than my queerly misruled reading of the conservators' sexuality may lodge in that *if*. If we follow the rule of the microscope — the instrument, in this episode, equivalent to the tape measure or ruler — we will aim for precision at the most infinitesimal scale, and we will be confident that we know what constitutes precision (and when and how to reject imprecision). Yet if instead we hold this perspective in tension with another — the one that stays with the dreamier logic of the teaser's evocative ambiguity rather than aiming to supersede it — then we may enjoy the pleasurably unruly sensation that comes from an equally unruly impression: all manner of fish and trees may be there, in the ether, for the detecting.

Map

The annals of mapmaking's history — and of mapmaking's often sinister embeddedness in colonial and imperial projects of unmaking and re-making the world — exists now at a scale that we might find staggering, bordering on overwhelming. Yet even a cursory glance at this history would bring starkly to the fore a sense of the map's dogged insistence, against the often glaring evidence to the contrary, that it achieves its ends of accuracy, of scaled proportionality, of neutrality. It would take only a similarly cursory glance at the history of television to grasp the genealogical connectedness of a proto-reality series like *This Old House* to a variety of contemporary reality series focused on houses and homes, including the multistranded *House Hunters* franchise (and especially its inflection as *House Hunters Renovation*). In this context, I am interested less in offering a thicker and denser description of that connectedness than in partially connecting the foregoing sections of this chapter to one conspicuous visual in the now ninety-plus-season run of *House Hunters International*: the animated neighborhood map to which we cut, in every episode, between live-action performances of house hunting, and on which are imaged the locations of three prospective houses that could be rented or purchased, alongside other elements of graphic design.

Unlike most maps (and of course there are other, intriguing exceptions that prove the rule of how maps ask us to understand that they work, when we think that they work), these *House Hunters International* inserts are aggressively — yet playfully — cartoonish. Just as a house-hunting couple approaches a coveted destination in a city center, so too do the map's two Gothic cathedrals approach the size of whole streets, crossing avenues. Or a homuncular cyclist dwarfs the route on which he makes his commute to the office, only to be dwarfed in turn by a leaf, signifying parkland. Or a tree is imaged at the same size as a cow or dog. And, time and again, enormous red thumbtacks drop thrice on each map to pin the "locations" (always hazily sketched) of prospective dwellings; in their outsized goofiness,

Fig. 5. *House Hunters International* (mis)maps Bordeaux. Source: Screen capture from *House Hunters International*.

the tacks remind me of nothing so much as the giant helmet that campily crushes Conrad at the top of *The Castle of Otranto* (eventually — inevitably — some flush expatriate client will appear in *House Hunters International* to buy, with the intention of restoring, a crumbling Italian castle). [See Figure 5.]

In such a context, the town square may come to feel more like a town quare. And, alongside that effect and others, these (in both senses) fabulous inserts may present themselves as (mis) mapping how we ought to read the series of which they form an integral part. The animations flirt with the mapmaker's pretensions to accuracy, proportion, and the like — only to depart fancifully and indeed giddily from such mapmaking norms, and to court our likewise, potentially giddy appreciation of the maneuver. In an analogous fashion, *House Hunters International* asks us at the top of every episode to assent to the fictions that serve as the series's governing principles and premises. Yet it winkingly allows us in on those principles' and premises' "real" status as ruses or sleights of hand — so that, for instance, it does not take much discernment (or Googling) to appreciate that the "three" houses imaged onscreen are just a few of many prospective houses that are or could be shown to clients; or that the clients have in fact already bought a house and the notion that they have seen "three" before making a decision on one is retrospectively manufactured; or that the difference in real estate preferences, manifesting as "conflict" in a couple formation, has been prepped, canned, and coached for the couple to perform and for their real estate agent to observe and navigate; or that the "real estate agent" showing that couple around a town or city is just a handsome actor paid to play a TV real estate agent; and on and on.

Does this lesson in (mis)mapping have a more global purchase beyond the local reading of *House Hunters International* — and at what scales or their slippage? Answering this question may allow a more explicit occasioning of the "building intensification and [...] spiraling involution" announced in this chapter's introduction, then worked for the most part implicitly over the course of its prior sections. By contrast, we could now map a playful, composite picture — provisional, and potentially ready for its own decomposing — and populate it with images, figures, and conceits otherwise encountered in the chapter...yet (re)scaled here to (mis)match the relative proportion or weight that each one of the images, figures, or conceits enjoyed before. At the center of the picture, place a mountain made of onions, and in adjacency, render a chef's knife and hands yet larger, looming over the mountain. In some corner, tuck a homuncular aerobicist, too large for the room in which he exercises — yet too small before the gigantic television screen whose fitness imperatives he follows. People some old house with rulers, oversized so that they fill the hallways they would usually measure, and landscape the house's yard with flowers yet bigger than the oversized rulers. Look at the picture not under a microscope but through a kaleidoscope, where the sizes and shapes of the picture's elements twist and morph and slide away. Call it *television*.

Interval

"And now," as *Monty Python* would have it, "for something completely different" (or will it turn out only to be partially so), I give you the Corpus of American Soap Operas, first as it is framed and described by linguist Mark Davies at his website, *BYU Corpora*:

> The SOAP corpus contains 100 million words of data from 22,000 transcripts [of] American soap operas from the early 2000s, and it serves as a great resource to look at very informal language.
>
> The corpus is related to many other corpora of English that we have created, which offer unparalleled insight into variation in English.
>
> Click on any of the links in the search form to the left for context-sensitive help, and to see the range of queries that the corpus offers. You might pay special attention to the (new) virtual corpora, which allow you to create personalized collections of texts related to a particular area of interest.[16]

Recognizing and appreciating the labor of Davies and his colleagues to create such a searchable corpus, I wish all the same that they had done more, in this framing and description, to recognize in turn the amount and kind of labor that preceded their own: namely, the anonymous work of numerous fans who created 22,000 complete transcripts of scripted dialogue, for every day's broadcast of over ten years' worth of all the then-airing serials in the American daytime programming bloc. When one clicks on the link that underscores the words, "22,000 transcripts," one lands on a chart of cumulative word counts headed with the neutral declaration, "The corpus is composed of 100,000,000 words in scripts from ten soap operas from 2001 [to] 2012." Only by then clicking on the link that underscores the word "scripts" does one arrive at the fan-curated and fan-maintained website — very different in look, tone, and feel — called, "Daytime Soap Transcripts from the TV MegaSite" (a title cap-

---

16 *Corpus of American Soap Operas,* https://www.english-corpora.org/soap/.

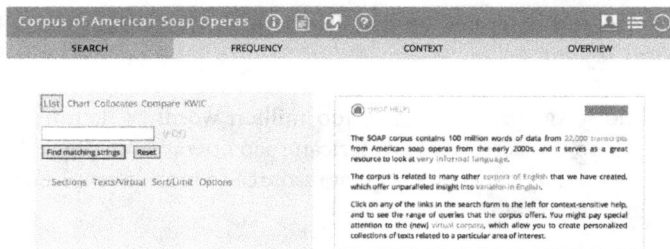

Fig. 6. The portal to the Corpus of American Soap Operas is unprepossessing. Source: Screen capture of website.

tioned with the much less neutral description, "TV Is Our Life") (Figures 6 and 7).[17]

In some way and to some extent, TV is my life, too; and though dwelling more closely and less partially with the MegaSite would prove fascinating, I will linger rather with the searchable corpus in order to take up its makers' invitation to cultivate "a particular area of interest." Searching for the word *scale,* I learn that it was used 303 times across the database's ten serials for the covered twelve-year period. Even a quick scan of the more detailed results, which quote the contexts in which the word uses appear, makes plain that the overwhelming majority of *scale*s inhabit the common phrase *scale of 1 to 10* or some more (and less) clever variants thereof. (As an aside, I find after my many viewings of *Family Feud,* to which I alluded earlier, that beginning a survey question with the phrase *on a scale of 1 to 10* is both one of the series' most common ways to frame a survey and easily its most common deployment of the word *scale*; the allied outcome in the serial, a form intimately connected historically to the game show, is not a surprising one.)

Playing further with this data opens onto ways of creating and undoing differently scaled intervals. First I give in to the

---

17   "Daytime Soap Transcripts from the TV MegaSite," *The TV MegaSite,*
     http://tvmegasite.net/day/transcripts.shtml.

Fig. 7. *The TV MegaSite* announces its fannish status visually. Source: Screen capture of website.

temptation to work meta-discursively and use a scale of 1 to 10 to count *scales of 1 to 10*: that is, I consult the first thirty entries in the — alphabetically organized — list of 303 search results for scale to see how many of them (twelve) or what percentage of them (40%) are *scales of 1 to 10* plus allied variants. To see what a sample covering a different interval may tell me, I count the same way just within and across the results for the year 2011 — and the percentage of *scales* that are also *scales of 1 to 10* (11 of 28 uses) is very strikingly close at 39%. This outcome may suggest the consistency of writing staffs' recourse to the common phrase, and it may invite further speculation about why this cliché has more of a grip on those industrial agents' imaginations than, say, *on a grand scale, on an international scale, on the Richter scale, (getting) on the (bathroom) scale, scale back, sliding scale,* and *scale a building* (constructions that also populate the list of search results enough times to be noticeable but not statistically noteworthy). Yet one could also adjust one's intervals of calculation and produce more statistical deviation than closeness in differentially reckoned uses of *scale of 1 to 10*. One version of that calculation that occurred to me involved counting all the uses of the phrase and variants first in the ABC serial *All My Children* and then in the serial *General Hospital,* likewise part of the ABC stable; in part, I made that move because, assessed in aesthetic, industrial, and historical registers, these two programs have arguably the most in common among the ten transcribed serials, and perhaps one could hypothesize that those commonalities extend to a facet of their construction scaled as small as one repeated phrasal unit. As it happens, they do not. Across the decade-plus of episodes, *All My Children* features 28 *scales of 1 to 10* out of 70 *scale* uses — coming in, by the bye, at exactly the 40% mark that was measured at other intervals. As for *General Hospital*, its 15 of 47 uses (about 32%) could be understood as constituting a significant statistical difference — as could the gap between *All My Children*'s versus *General Hospital*'s total uses of the word *scale* (23% versus about 15-and-a-half%).

If you made it to the end of the preceding paragraph without having your eyes glaze over, you deserve a cookie, a medal, or both. Hardly at this point in *Television Scales* will you be surprised to know that I am agnostic about the recent trend in the humanities to mine data in the service of textual and cultural analysis. Indeed, so micro-scaled do I regard the interval between the first two, consonantly according versions of number-crunching that I performed and the third, "disturbance"-yielding one, that the performance leaves me craving a more wholesale derangement or short-circuiting of such an effort. And then I wonder whether that more perverse move could retain, if to deform, some sense of scale as interval rather than simply set it aside. Whatever value it yields, perhaps pleasure would come from the move if it were enacted as a collaging together of *scale*-featuring dialogues from the transcripts, in a way that would make a found poem — one that not only offers up a flavor or intimation of how twenty-first-century daytime *sounded* for a spell but that also stitches its words together in scaled intervals of citation.

* * *

There's an enormous difference in scale between infidelity and murder.

Yeah, but on the life scale, there aren't very many "things like this." So if you do want to talk,

be honest. How angry are you with me for not telling you about Griffin, on a scale from one to punching my lights out? *I'm not angry. Okay? I understand why you didn't tell me. It's all good. Hey, you helped keep my brother alive. Yes, you did. Thank you.*

I just need to know how you overcome the unforgivable. Is there some forgivability scale that I missed out on? Like, say, you sleeping with your stepfather would be a 4 out of— Hey, that is not how it works. *Well, then tell me how it works. Please. Please, if you could just tell me how you convinced Jason to forgive you, well, then maybe I can figure out a way for Lucky to forgive me, too.* Oh, okay. Um,

use water from the Snyder pond as the primary source of irrigation. Now while a pond may be adequate for the maintenance of a family farm, how do you propose to scale it for multiple unit usage? *Well, that's a*

blending together, a little bit, and I honestly don't know where I land on that scale. Of good and bad,

you are very good at this. Mm-hmm. On a scale.

Ladder

As has been well-documented (and lamented), the years in which fans transcribed daytime serial dialogue were twilight ones for the genre; of the ten serials populating the database described above, only four continue to air, and many suspect that the days of those final four are numbered. Yet over the course of the same period that witnessed the waning of daytime serials' popularity and the cancellation of most of them, the melodramatizing and serializing of just about every other form of narrative storytelling in American television — an intensification and extension of a process begun in the late 1970s and early 1980s — diffused and suffused on a massive scale those serials' influence (however oblique) and legacy (however under-acknowledged, especially in the realm of so-called "quality" television). One paradigmatic locus of the seep of melodrama and seriality into a manifold number of formal containers is also the object of this chapter's final section: the three-season Hulu Original series, *The Path*. The series also capitalizes on a trend, begun in premium cable in the 1990s and then extended exponentially in basic cable and beyond, to continue to foreground narrative television's obsession with the nuclear family — yet to ring a change on that obsession by representing the family's dark and messy imbrication with worlds of organized crime (*The Sopranos, Ozark*), drug dealing (*Weeds, Breaking Bad, Claws*), secret polygamist sects of unofficial Mormonism (*Big Love*), and more.

In the case of *The Path*, the nuclear family are Eddie and Sarah Lane and their children, and the dark world to which they belong is the cult of Meyerism, whose main compound and central headquarters are adjacent to the sleepy town in upstate New York where the Lanes reside. Precisely because *The Path* participates in a television tradition of serialized storytelling, it discloses information about how the cult works (or fails to work) and how pernicious it is (or not) in gradual, punctual, accretive ways. Starting with the pilot, we learn that the two organizing metaphors for Meyerism are The Light and The Ladder. Meyerists feel the love, warmth, and radiance of The Light ever more richly and intensely through an ascent of The Ladder, a set of teachings and experiences whose rungs indicate spiritual growth and development.[18] Except — as this narrative centers on a cult, after all, and as we come to understand incrementally and over time — the Meyerists take the metaphors literally and believe that their hand-burning founder climbed a ladder made of fire to reach The Light; that The Light will shine permanently

---

18 Jessica Goldberg, "What the Fire Throws," *The Path*, Hulu (original release date: March 30, 2016).

in The Garden that exists beyond the earthly realm; that tending the diminished version of The Garden in the here and now is a rehearsal for an eventual, full ascent of The Ladder, which the enlightened will undertake when non-Meyerists' evil and corruption become so overwhelming that they initiate an apocalypse; and on and on.

As viewers come to understand this structuring mythos with more and more seeming completion — chiefly through flashback and through dialogue that informs us about the cult's founding and initial efflorescence — they may sense that they are also scaling a kind of parallel ladder and feel the concomitant satisfaction of acquiring narrative knowledge (in this meta-melodramatic instance, knowledge that is — reflexively — sentimentalized and sensationalized). Yet they may also feel knocked off the ladder, or at least knocked down a few rungs, as the retrospective tendency of the series collides jarringly, and deliberately, with its forward-driving narrative momentums and propulsions. Indeed, the more time passes and the more we experience of "what happens" to the Lanes and company, we also discover that "what happened" to create and cement the existence of the cult in the 1970s and 80s forms no stable backstory to be nostalgically invoked by the cult's champions; rather, it is composed of and as an irreducibly complex agon played out among a variety of likewise complex actors, and that agon is increasingly, intensively subject to contestation and revisionary reframing. In other words — and, in this way, the borrowings from daytime serials and their earliest primetime imitators are acute — "what happened" was always already an up-and-down version of "what happens" now and what will happen in the future; or, to borrow Ien Ang's classic formulation, open-ended television melodrama like and including *The Path* is fundamentally "characterized by an endless fluctuation between happiness and unhappiness," which positions "life [as] a question of falling down and getting up again."[19] *The Path* invokes the idea of suc-

---

19 Ien Ang, *Watching Dallas: Soap Opera and the Melodramatic Imagination,* trans. Della Couling (New York: Routledge, 1985), 45.

cess in scaling the ladder vividly and repeatedly, conveying both its ongoing power as a motor of fantasy and pleasure and its ongoing incommensurability for understanding "falling down and getting up again," by which I mean (partially) understanding the connections among families, communities, and their discontents; among past, present, and future.

* * *

Scaling down and back from a synoptic overview of *The Path* to a closer look at its component parts, I find heuristic value in one of television studies' oft-repeated truisms: namely, that the second episode of a series will tell and show one much more about its repeatable premises, ethos, and mechanics than the pilot, which aims to accomplish the different goal of launching (and selling) the work. I also find, in re-viewing the second episode of *The Path*, that it televises with an astonishing uncanniness (should I subscribe, after all, to The Light?) the animating concepts and concerns of this chapter of *Television Scales* and the foregoing one.[20] Ashley's account of feeling "burdened — like, weighted down" previews the myriad ways in which the Meyerists cultivate techniques for what they call, by contrast, "unburdening." Believed to have had an extramarital affair, unruly Eddie is ruled by his spiritual guide in "the movement" to submit to a period of solitary reflection, measured precisely (on the basis of ongoing Meyerist experimentation and tweaking) to last for fourteen days. Cal pursues ambitions, including an appearance in a local television news segment, to get Meyerism more fully "on the map," that is, to map the movement more broadly and thus expand the scale of its success and profitability. Intervals of time — the time between Eddie's trip to Peru and his meeting of a "Former" (Meyerist jargon for abandoners of the cult), the time between the Former's husband's passing and the conclusion of her cross-country drive to see grandparents

---

20 Jessica Goldberg, "The Era of the Ladder," *The Path*, Hulu (original release date: March 30, 2016).

from whom the cult estranged her, her sixteen-year time in the cult — invite our speculation about how they calibrate (or not) with each other.

Simultaneously, and for the most part, no one is successfully scaling ladders in this episode. Teenaged Hawk is flopping in his navigation of the path between home life in the cult and sociality at high school. Sarah is flipping out about Eddie's untrustworthiness. Mary purges elements of her abusive past — en route to a joint binge of banal Meyerist aphorisms and of sex with Cal. Meanwhile, Cal is in the throes of a bad ego trip and of an errant plan for Meyerism, whereas Eddie becomes turned on to what truth looks like beyond the cult's watchful eye, literalized in the giant eye-shaped icons that pervade the spaces of Meyerism. When Cal promises — or threatens — to multiply the number and reach of these eyes, and as that forecast coincides nearly and neatly with his proselytizing "on" the local news, *The Path* begets a question, a remainder for further installments of the series as well as for this chapter: when and how is television watching us?

Suturing "The TV Studies Sutras"

Headnote

Dodie Bellamy's *The TV Sutras* is a dividual book of unequal parts: (1) seventy-eight sutras, transcriptions of language heard in television broadcasts, which are accompanied by commentaries that gloss them, followed by (2) a long personal essay, describing itself sometimes as a novel, in which Bellamy writes her first extended, confessional account of the ten years that she was "lost" in a cult. The essay is also (pardon, as you will see, the pun) a meditation on the interval between Bellamy's time in the cult and her life now in San Francisco — and what it positions her to philosophize about some ideas that we have likewise encountered in *Television Scales* (charisma, complexity), some that have yet to enjoy the same level of attention (sincerity, the master con).

Sincerity, and the possibility that it is painfully cringe-worthy, is also explored in Bellamy's short headnote, "The Source of the Transmission," which follows the first part of the book's epigraph (Krishnamurti: *"Truth is a pathless land"* — but a *Pathless* one?) and precedes the sutras themselves.[1] That headnote's admission of the risk of sincerity culminates a paragraph that

---

1   Dodie Bellamy, *The TV Sutras* (Brooklyn: Ugly Duckling Presse, 2014), 11.

begins with Bellamy's explanation of how she composed the book's first part:

> In receiving the TV *Sutras,* I attuned myself to messages that are broadcast into the living room of my San Francisco apartment. My method: I do a half-hour yoga set while watching the DVD *Peaceful Weight Loss through Yoga.* Then I turn off the DVD player and TV, sit cross-legged on the floor, facing the television, and meditate for twenty minutes. [...] When I finish meditating, I crawl off my cushion and turn the TV back on. Words and images emerge. There's a flash of recognition and my hand scribbles furiously: I transcribe the first words that strike me, then briefly I describe the scene from which the TV sutra arose. I take a breath, scoot against the wall and quickly write my commentary. Sometimes my interpretation surprises me. Sometimes I disagree with it. But I write down whatever comes. I do not attempt irony, cleverness or perfection — or art. The TV *Sutras* are totally in-the-moment sincere, even if that sincerity makes me cringe afterwards.[2]

As the reader turns from this headnote to the sutras and commentaries, she will, *pace* the headnote's apologia, find moments of evident irony, cleverness, and artfulness, as well as passages that seem unvarnished: sincere without putting *sincere* in scarequotes. Is Bellamy, then, trying to con us in the headnote when she says that the sutras are "totally in-the-moment sincere"? And how can we tell?

These questions are not quite meant to be answered, because Bellamy's overall strategy in *The TV Sutras* — of which the first instance in the headnote is a synecdochic representative — is to leave us globally uncertain about truth's relationship to fiction, not just locally uncertain regarding sincerity and its obversions. Beyond their sincerity or its occlusion, were the sutras actually composed according to the method that Bellamy describes? Was she really in a cult for ten years, or is the seemingly memoiristic

---

2   Ibid., 14.

essay that comprises the book's second part a wholesale fabrication? Again, Bellamy is canny and deliberative about wanting — at least a first-time — reader of the book not to be able to make conclusive answers to these questions during the phenomenal, beat-to-beat reading of the book (and hopefully, I believe she would aver, its charisma will seduce the reader to read the book in one sitting without putting it down). If, afterward, that reader discovered online an essay-length exposé that Bellamy wrote, some time earlier than *The TV Sutras,* about the cult Eckankar, then it would be a short walk from that discovery to a set of "keys" for reading the essay: the unnamed cult of the essay is indeed an account of Eckankar, or ECK; the cult leader whom the essay's narrator describes as her "Master" closely matches other accounts of Eckankar's Darwin Gross, who was eventually forced out of his leadership role in the cult; Gross released an album called *It Just Is!* — rendered as *The Sound of Spirit* in the essay; a high-ranking member of the cult, Neva Novak, who claims to hail from Jupiter, appears in the essay as a translation of ECK's Omnec Onec, who claims to hail from Venus; and on and on. Yet, fascinating a rabbit-hole as this one is to slide down, that eventual sliding takes nothing away from, and is perhaps wrongheadedly at odds with, the end toward which Bellamy is driving the uncertainties and instabilities that animate her text: namely, to give us a sensorial and affective experience of, and not just a didactic argument about, what it feels like to flip and flop inside a con...that maybe isn't a con...but that *must* be a con...but that isn't, right?

In this way, what Bellamy demonstrates, indeed theatricalizes, about cults (and, as she makes plain, cults as one period-specific manifestation of what she takes all religions to do) connects her estimation of them, much less partially than, say, puns on *transmission* and *receiver,* to estimations we may likewise make about television. Television, like religious or cult teaching, is full of banality, clichés, and lies; television, like those teachings, blends fact and fiction uneasily; yet television and such teaching also have in common seductive appeals and, harder for one to swallow when one is committed to critique, conditional access to truth and poignancy. So, too, Bellamy, as she well understands by using television words and images in the first place, and as she figures herself authorially in the book's first part. There, in the complex swirl of tones that animate the sutras and their commentaries — sutured together at times with delicate humor, pulsing at times with gestures toward barely submerged or displaced critique — Bellamy gives us truth and lie, banal cliché and poignant moments. And she does so charmingly.

* * *

Like Bellamy's own headnote, this one frames a series of writings, "The TV Studies Sutras," that I have produced in homage to her. Every day for a month in 2018, I meditated for twenty minutes in the afternoon. Next I turned to some work in television studies, flipping pages quickly and scanning words without overthinking until I alighted on the passage that announced itself to me as the day's sutra. Then I wrote the accompanying commentaries to which the sutras are sutured, likewise quickly and without overthinking. They now follow this headnote's final cut, and they will in their turn be followed by (once more, pardon the pun) a meditation on cuts: as sutures, and as formal elements that, among other partially connective qualities, unite Bellamy and Strathern.

* * *

1
September 1, 2018

Sutra
"In all developed broadcasting systems the characteristic organisation, and therefore the characteristic experience, is one of sequence or flow. This phenomenon, of planned flow, is then

perhaps the defining characteristic of broadcasting, simultaneously as a technology and as a cultural form."[3]

Commentary
Unlike in meditation, to go with the flow of television is to be insufficiently critical. Television should be read as closely — and as broadly — as television studies is read: here, notice the simultaneity of flow's structuring of technology, irreducibly complex at one scale, and of cultural form, irreducibly complex at another. As with the broadcasting phenomenon, which may be paradoxically, simultaneously scale-slipping and scale-maintaining, so too the work of the word *simultaneously* here, which asks us at once to appreciate the distinction in order and register of technology and of cultural form and to conceptualize the fractal coincidence of flow's organization of each of these elements of television.

2
September 2, 2018

Sutra
"The usual episodic character of television only gives the illusion of continuity by offering series consisting of twenty-six individual units. The series may continue over a period of years, revolving around the actions of a set of regular characters. As pointed out, however, there is no sense of continuous involvement with these characters. They have no memory. They cannot change in response to events that occur within a weekly installment, and consequently they have no history."[4]

---

3   Raymond Williams, *Television: Technology and Cultural Form* (London and New York: Routledge Classics, 2003), 86.

4   Horace Newcomb, TV: *The Most Popular Art* (Garden City: Anchor Press, 1974), 253–54.

Commentary

Have the classic characters of sitcoms, procedurals, Westerns, and the like been conferred the slippery gift to which the student of meditation aspires, perpetually? Being in the now, wholly of the moment, do they enact pure consciousness without having to intone their mantras? Or what but degraded mantras are these series' incessantly repeated gestures, facial mugs, gag lines, tag lines, and catchphrases? Like the lure of transcendence, they promise to take us "to the moon!" Yet we hear the violence in that promise, the threat that it really constitutes, coming at it from the dark side of the moon: remembering, tending histories, not occulting ourselves at the foreshortened scale of the episode but cultivating the expanded, serial life.

3
September 3, 2018

Sutra

"Television is itself a major agency for the daily enactment of that 'common co-existence of cleavage and continuity'. Its modes of presentation are derived from both dominant and subordinate codes, and the tension between different sectors of society is actually *enacted* — not so much in the denotative content of the messages as in the way those messages are presented."[5]

Commentary

Cleavage may be contrasted with continuity. Yet, corrugated and involute, a cleavage may itself be understood as dividual: a cleavage from something and, at the same time, a cleavage to that thing. In cleaving to and from television, do we subordinate ourselves to it, and are we also trying to dominate it? What is the mode of our enactments before, behind, and beyond screens? Tensile in my sensate engagements with television, I may appear

---

5   John Westergaard and Henrietta Resler, *Class in a Capitalist Society* (Harmondsworth: Penguin, 1976), 7, qtd. in John Fiske and John Hartley, *Reading Television* (London: Routledge, 2003), 112.

quite still as I tune in — maybe even as still as the meditator also tuning in to one frequency or another — yet my inner eye could be a major agency, moving across different scales of encodement as if moving across different sectors of an (inevitably) classed, capitalist society.

4

September 4, 2018

Sutra
"Even bestsellers reaching several million readers touch only a small percentage of the total population. If the scale of magnitude by which television audiences are measured were applied to these bestsellers, even they would not rate publication, let alone serious novels and books of poetry or philosophy, which sell in numbers too small to be noticeable on the scale used for TV audiences."[6]

Commentary
When the scale-upsetting multiplication of television forces, forms, and forums rhymes with their fragmentation and dispersal, a de-scaling of the expectations for popularity and the metrics for success also obtains. Out of the Bunker, into the niche. If we can no longer speak or write of "the age of television" as an era defined saturatingly and saturatedly by television as technology and as cultural form, but rather must reckon with the *age* of television as its slides ever further into its lateness and belatedness, we can also look to ageing television for vital poetry and lively philosophy — as well as for the a-poetic and the anti-philosophical. But we can look backward, too, carefully opening our eyes wider and wider, as we are blasted forward with thunderous speed; and if, so looking, we examine forgotten corners and forlorn crevices of television past and television passed, what

---

6   Martin Esslin, *The Age of Television* (San Francisco: W.H. Freeman and Company, 1982), 91–92.

missed poetry and mistook philosophy will we comprehend was in the tube all along, waiting to be filtered from the static?

5
September 5, 2018

Sutra
"Twice a week, three times a week, five times a week, the familiar signature tune alerts us to the fact that the serial is about to begin. It does not disappear 'until the autumn' or 'until the next series.'"[7]

Commentary
Waiting for autumn to come — and, with it, first the bursts of color and then the falling of the leaves — I am already mournful for all the canceled serials of my youth. Like sophisticated rulers, they measured the intricate passage of time, its weathers and its whethers. The rock star asks in her signature tune, "Can I handle the seasons of my life," and I picture her addressing the dozens of suffering serial women parading across the screen. *The Seasons of My Life* would make a splendid name for the kind of programming that is no longer commissioned for American daytime television — and from which the under-acknowledged borrowings are so wholly yet ethereally diffused across the primetime landscape that they are impossible to map. Without the ruler of yesteryear, without the impossible map, we prick our ears and hope to hear, as if falling from the sky, the strains of some familiar, comforting song.

---

7   Christine Geraghty, "The Continuous Serial — A Definition," *Coronation Street*, ed. Richard Dyer (London: BFI, 1981), 9–10.

6
September 6, 2018

Sutra

"Fantasy is therefore a fictional area which is relatively cut off and independent. It does not function in place of, but beside, other dimensions of life (social practice, moral or political consciousness). It is a dimension of subjectivity which is a source of pleasure *because* it puts 'reality' in parentheses, because it constructs imaginary solutions for real contradictions which in their fictional simplicity and their simple fictionality step outside the tedious complexity of the existing social relations of dominance and subordination."[8]

Commentary

"I look at you, and I fantasize: you're mine tonight," I could sing in time with the terrible — which is to say, delightful — music video, if *you* would mean the light of the TV screen and *mine* would mean immersion in its glow. Could a version of immersion be achieved, so fantastically pleasurable and pleasingly fantasmatic, that I would really feel cut off, hovering in another dimension? In that suture, the irreducible complexity of existing social relations would have no place or space. And place itself would be nothing more than the only vaguely discernible location of a breath; space would liquefy into dimly perceptible color and sound. Floating into entrancement would not count me a feminist, but it also would not count against me in return to "reality" (is it "really" in parentheses, or does its literal scare-quoting, not identical with parenthetical aside-making, bracket it in some other, relative way?).

8   Ien Ang, *Watching Dallas: Soap Opera and the Melodramatic Imagination*, trans. Della Couling (London and New York: Methuen, 1985), 135.

7
September 7, 2018

Sutra
"The network anchor is a very special variety of star — subdued, constructed through reduction and simplification, and authorized to speak the truth. The influence of the 'evening star' seems personal, but it is really positional."[9]

Commentary
Decades ago, television studies found rightly needful the imperative to identify technical, cultural, and ideological constructions, to trace their contours with great care and detail so that, grasped thus, they could be grappled with. The study of television *still* needs versions of this work, but now the work must proceed in the baleful context in which the best journalists lack deserved support, while the worst leaders' cults are full of passionate followers. I wish reality television had been given a different name — and one more aggressively sutured from reality than "reality" in scare quotes. Along with the wish, a hope: that it is not narcissistic to have just read and taken solace from some of my own writing about where and when a positionality may take on the character of an oppositionality. An astute friend takes to social media to rebrand and recast the creepiest cult guru of them all, the one about whom we hear that he hates dogs, as the "abuser in chief"; while a gag gift from my mother-in-law, a tea towel, is emblazoned with the catchphrase, "My cat would make a better president." That is a fact.

---

9   Margaret Morse, "The Television News Personality and Credibility: Reflections on the News in Transition," in *Studies in Entertainment: Critical Approaches to Mass Culture,* ed. Tania Modleski (Bloomington and Indianapolis: Indiana University Press, 1986), 59.

8
September 8, 2018

Sutra

"For many intellectuals historically leery of entertaining machines of pleasure, TV is just too banal an object. Or, when faced
with television, their response is akin to Jack Gould's comment
(quoted by Boddy) that after one episode of a quiz show or a
Western, he had nothing else to say. The aim of this book is
'to change the object itself,' transforming TV into a theoretical
object."[10]

Commentary

When regarded from the right angles and for the right aspects,
television is an eminently, stunningly theoretical object. It opens
itself up, then, not for banal theory but for the theorization of
banality, as well as for theoretically inflected challenges to the
supposed banality of its objecthood. Hear the words *entertaining machines of pleasure* two ways: machines of pleasure are entertaining; and we should make time and space to entertain machines of pleasure, thereby understanding their circuits, levers,
gears, and coils. All of those descriptors may be taken literally,
metaphorically, or both at once. And television may be taken
not only for its objecthood but also for its generative subject-
hood. Whether pleasurably, painfully, or otherwise — and trans-
formatively, ever — it emits, it implants, it installs. We come to
it, and it becomes us.

---

10 Roland Barthes, "Change the Object Itself," in *Image-Music-Text,* trans.
    Stephen Heath (New York: Hill and Wang, 1977), 165, qtd. in Patricia Mel-
    lencamp, "Prologue," in *Logics of Television: Essays in Cultural Criticism,*
    ed. Patricia Mellencamp (Bloomington and Indianapolis: Indiana Univer-
    sity Press, 1990), 12.

9
September 9, 2018

Sutra

"Requiring upper middle class status as a mark of normalcy creates a world that forces black viewers to accept a value system in which they are the inevitable losers. A value system based upon social class (upper equals good, lower equals bad: a notion with a sinister Orwellian ring) devalues most black people, for whom a high-income life-style like the Huxtables' is quite unattainable. Black viewers are thus caught in a trap because the escape route from TV stereotyping comes with a set of ideologically loaded conditions."[11]

Commentary

Whether in *1984* or 1984, the loser feels the sinister as sting or slap or stop. Her black life matters, if only the expensive clothing chosen by the sitcom's wardrobe department would reflect that mattering. But asking to be reflected is a dangerous game to play in, with, and through a medium whose simultaneously miniaturizing and giganticizing screen is almost always a funny house mirror. Misrecognition is the signature code, misrule the signal scale. But then again, onscreen come slender moments, subtle zigs, sudden zags, and dwelling delicately inside them, a viewer feels between herself and her putative television avatar a proportion so synced that gratification soars and swells. Its ambiguous aftermath: the churning of a desire that by its nature cannot be fulfilled, another kind of trap from which no escape route discloses itself other than uneasily.

---

11 Sut Jhally and Justin Lewis, "Enlightened Racism: *The Cosby Show,* Audiences and the Myth of the American Dream," in *The Audience Studies Reader,* eds. William Brooker and Deborah Jermyn (New York: Routledge, 2002), 280.

10
September 10, 2018

Sutra

"The approaches represented here begin with the belief that relationships between viewer and television are so complex and multidimensional that they resist all attempts to reduce them to phenomena that can be explained by the same procedures that work for the chemist."[12]

Commentary

If not chemists, then alchemists? How to make gold of the output that is television studies, especially when, our capacious understanding of the relationships between viewer and television notwithstanding, we take a look at some of our inputs and find them particularly dull or drossy? And can we be good alchemists if we are at the same time compelled, as if following a laboratory procedure, to keep intoning the mantra about the irreducible complexity that obtains at every scale of television phenomenality and materiality? Today I have more questions than answers, but my meditation practice encourages me to be untroubled by the experience of doubt and worry, which — perhaps here is an alchemical transformation — could also become an experience of wonder over television, over television studies, over the sutras that come to me in little waves and sometimes little earthquakes.

11
September 11, 2018

Sutra

"Since the inhabitants of critical discourse cannot avoid the intellectual work of audience-creation, let it be explicitly creative,

---

12   Robert C. Allen, "Introduction to the Second Edition, More Talk about TV," *Channels of Discourse, Reassembled: Television and Contemporary Criticism,* ed. Robert C.Allen, 2nd edn. (New York: Routledge, 1992), 16.

and not hidden behind the fiction of a 'real' audience that's always located somewhere beyond the critical activity itself."[13]

Commentary
Reader, I am making you up. But don't worry about it; I'm kind to my creations. I don't think you're a monster itching to write a bad review on Amazon, a distracted multitasker who isn't reading closely enough, a zombie who's just flipping through the pages to see the next screen capture. I am making you in my image, and I have an abundance of self-regard. And yet, regarding you (in both senses), I do not think to make you work. I let you be.

12
September 12, 2018

Sutra
"It is not a question, finally, of understanding simply television's ideological (or representational) role, or simply its ritual (or socially organizing) function, or the process of its domestic (and more broadly social) consumption. It is a question of how to understand all these issues (or dimensions) in relation to each other."[14]

Commentary
To scale, or not to scale? That *is* the question. Like a number of profoundly secular atheists I know, I make a ritual of reading various versions of my online horoscope throughout the morning and the afternoon, organizing my time — through a kind of dayparting — with predictions, advice, and other banalities. Coincidentally, mine is the sign of the scales. I can share that datum, though my mantra is "secret" — but you can figure it out

---

13 John Hartley, "The Real World of Audiences," in *Tele-ology: Studies in Television* (London and New York: Routledge, 1992), 123.

14 David Morley, *Television, Audiences and Cultural Studies* (London and New York: Routledge, 1992), 276.

if you know the year of my birth and of my teacher's training. Two non-representational syllables, two ideologically overdetermined years, my domestic consumption of words and images on my smartphone and computer screens, the broad planets, the social gods: how should I understand all these partial issues (or partial dimensions) in relation to each other? Scooby-Doo, where on heaven or earth are you?

13
September 13, 2018

Sutra
"Television programs not only transmit therapeutic strategies taken from the world of psychological theory and clinical practice but also construct new therapeutic relationships."[15]

Commentary
I confess: I survived childhood abuse with television as a therapist. *Knots Landing* was the best clinician, allegorizing my victimization and my fighting back in ways I did not properly understand when I was eleven, but *Roseanne* was also a boon and a salve. So when *Roseanne* came back from the television grave, and before Roseanne and "Roseanne" got justly ushered back there, I found an awkward and partial catharsis in bearing witness to scenes of Roseanne and Darlene on the Conner couch — symbol, icon, and prosthetic prop, all at once. My mother votes deplorably, too, yet she has not had the capacity (or the opportunity) to give a good hug in quite a long while. Cut to a music video: "My therapist says not to see her no more."

---

15   Mimi White, *Tele-Advising: Therapeutic Discourse in American Television* (Chapel Hill: University of North Carolina Press, 1992), 19.

14
September 14, 2018

Sutra
"In a similar way, *Laverne and Shirley* (1976–83) often developed its lesbian narratives and queer pleasures by 'passing through' heterosexuality and other forms of relationships with men in order to reestablish the emotional and erotic status quo of two women living and working together. Much of the audience pleasure in this series is bound up in seeing how various threats to maintaining Laverne and Shirley as a couple are overcome."[16]

Commentary
"We'll do it our way." Yes, our queer way. If the way involves finding what we have pleasurably hoped and expected to find, then at least sometimes we owe that gift to its having been placed by some industrial agent or agents right where we knew to look for it, hiding in plain sight. Television: a glass closet. Television: a strict enforcer and gleeful breaker of heteronormative law — although I would not like an episode in which Laverne goes to bed with a cop. If she does have to pass through the precinct of heterosexuality to find her way home to lesbian heaven, let the route be peopled with handymen instead. Dear producers, when designing women, remember that we like to see them live together, and we like to see them work together, and if we can see those status quos coincide, then it's double the pleasure, double the fun.

---

16 Alexander Doty, *Making Things Perfectly Queer: Interpreting Mass Culture* (Minneapolis: University of Minnesota Press, 1993), 51.

15
September 15, 2018

Sutra
"The geotelevisual system does not merely facilitate consumption of commodities but produces a substance of value all its own: socialized culture time."[17]

Commentary
If it's six o'clock in the evening, it's time to play *Family Feud* and then to cook family dinner. If Valene's identity starts to dissociate, it's time to roast the Thanksgiving turkey. If spring cleaning is overdue, it's time for May sweeps. If…but by and large, these are *if*s of another century's television. Reruns are now confined to narrow channels, appointment viewing is for the middle-aged and elderly, and if it isn't streaming, it is not only not in my students' flow but also persists at a smaller scale in the field from which the coming teachers' sutras will be drawn. Sometimes I wish that they could come more slowly; that chasing after theory after television was less a chase, less a scramble, more an amble; that, with television and with theory, I could still have more still life in more real time.

16
September 16, 2018

Sutra
"Of course, these very contradictions — the multitude of differences within what's been dismissed as television's vast sea of indifference — prevents us from selecting any one case as the representative one. Nonetheless, some texts seem to me to be

---

17 Richard Dienst, *Still Life in Real Time: Theory after Television* (Durham: Duke University Press, 1994), xi.

particularly instructive in considering television's relationship to discourses of gender (both on TV and about it)."[18]

Commentary

"Joan Van Arking" is a term that was dubbed in the television industry to describe the way a "difficult" diva performs — with the collateral lesson that the best thing one can do in such cases, if part of the camera crew, lighting department, or the like, is to stay out of her way (it's always *her* way), let her do her thing, and hope for the best in attempting to capture it in one or another take. Have I been Joan Van Arking lately? Are my high standards and keen demands — of myself, of others, of television, of television studies, of the sutras — "too much"? Maybe it's time to channel the alternate excess of my inner Donna Mills and echo her sing-along to the one-hit-wonder's hit: "Don't worry, be happy." At the same time, as with any mantra, I shouldn't cling to it but hear it lightly, let it come and go. Melodramatic womanhood is no one thing. Its multitude of differences doesn't merely erupt across putatively representative case studies but within them, too.

17
September 17, 2018

Sutra

"Talk shows not only promote conversation and debate, they break down the distance between the audience and the stage. They do not depend on the power or expertise of bourgeois education. They elicit common sense and everyday experience as the mark of truth. They confound the distinction between the public and private. Talk shows are about average women as citizens talking about and debating issues and experience."[19]

---

18 Lynn Joyrich, *Re-Viewing Reception: Television, Gender, and Postmodern Culture* (Bloomington: Indiana University Press, 1996), 41.

19 Jane M. Shattuc, "The Oprahification of America: Talk Shows and the Public Sphere," in *Television, History, and American Culture: Feminist Critical*

Commentary
You may want to talk about Oprah, but consider the time that Omnec Onec appears in *The Jerry Springer Show*. Far from average, she is a stunning blonde beauty and claims to be a multi-hundred-year-old Venusian who has temporarily assumed human form. It's true that her charisma doesn't depend on bourgeois education — but she also claims a longer, higher, and deeper education in the halls of her native planet's single domed city. Ice in her eyes and caged and cagy restraint in her voice, she creates a bracing fourth wall between herself on stage and Jerry and the audience on its other side. She is not really, she explains, a citizen of the United States, nor even of the earthly realm. If she breaks down the distinction between the public and private, she does so unwittingly. We have to understand that her internationally circulating book (she's big in Germany), with its hackneyed public message of peace and love, has a painful, private subtext of childhood abuse and trauma, dissociation, and thus the embrace, the fantasizing, of another world.

18
September 18, 2018

Sutra
"This book should serve as a siren — one that incites action. That action might take the form of self-interrogation, change of career, critical debate, or screaming in the streets. Whatever the response, critical contemplation and action are needed to stop the nihilism informing the treatment, evaluation of, and prolific visual representation of Black women's actual and fictionalized bodies."[20]

    Essays, eds. Mary Beth Haralovich and Lauren Rabinovitz (Durham: Duke University Press, 1999), 171.
20 Beretta Smith-Shomade, *Shaded Lives: African-American Women and Television* (New Brunswick: Rutgers University Press, 2002), 7.

Commentary

This sutra should serve as a siren — whether you take that assertion to mean that the ambulance is justly speeding the bruised and battered body to the emergency room, or that the sweet, seductive voice is calling the men who steer the ship to annihilation: also justly. The men's nihilism leads to a different kind of annihilation of different kinds of subjects, raced, gendered, and classed otherwise, living the paradox of marginalization and disappearance even as (and because) they are ushered spectacularly into view. These days, as in others, a stunning amount of screaming in the streets gets televised, sometimes stirringly… but often in the frame of damaging, disturbing misprision. Will television deliver us from evil — or straight into the gaping maw of its devilish star?

19
September 19, 2018

Sutra

"If there are to be more Tiananmens and fewer 11 Septembers, the viewers of today and tomorrow must have a wide range of pleasurable, smart, progressive TV programmes to look at, learn from, and influence."[21]

Commentary

Of course give your money to PBS, and enjoy your tote bag and your access to Thirteen's partial online archive. But how not only to help public service television to survive but also to restore the slenderly glimpsed, radical promise that could have been its lot? How to generate new versions of beautiful "old" programming — like the sadly shortlived *Soul!* — for the old "new" medium that is now our television? For starters, I want my FCC. I dream of harnessing the voting power of all the viewers of *The*

---

21   Toby Miller, "Preface," in *Television Studies,* ed. Toby Miller (London: BFI, 2002), vii.

Voice who come close, but almost always never close enough, to giving beautiful, soulful black divas the win.

20
September 20, 2018

Sutra
"Television — once the most familiar of everyday objects — is now transforming at such rapid speeds that we no longer really know what 'TV' is at all."[22]

Commentary
The familiarity that television used to have was always the strange, estranged familiarity that we most commonly denote as *uncanny*. One need only conjure a memory of its weird houses to savor that uncanny flavor. As for the relation of that then of uncanny television to whatever it is "now," I shared this observation with friends at the time of the initial airing of the *Twin Peaks* revival, *Twin Peaks: The Return*: "I gave up a long time ago on Lynch's television project, so, no, I am not an informed commentator who slogged through eighteen summer hours of his latest TV business. But I remember the first season keenly and mournfully (though precisely not nostalgically), and I watched the last few minutes of the sequel with real interest and curiosity. And I think they make perfect and splendid sense to anyone who has clocked about this series/these series that they are fundamentally preoccupied with the unfinished and unfinishable *work* that trauma creates, creates again, and creates 'one' more time for the people who have, without choice, to tarry with trauma — especially in its more discrete forms as abuses and their legacies. And the suburban house is a goddamned magnet and lightning rod for that work."

---

22 Lynn Spigel, "Introduction," in *Television after TV: Essays on a Medium in Transition*, eds. Lynn Spigel and Jan Olsson (Durham: Duke University Press, 2004), 6.

21

September 21, 2018

Sutra
"The interdisciplinary scope of the project has generated a need to imagine television not only as a site of commercial entertainment but as a site of military intelligence and scientific observation as well. Decades of satellite uses have shaped not only *what we see on television* but also *how we understand what 'television' is and means.*"[23]

Commentary
If I were an archaeologist, or an astronomer, or a geographer, how would I look at "television," and what would I think it means? With a weak and a lazy mind, I have been spending too much time instead on questions borne from astrology, and everybody knows what Adorno would think about that. All the same, value erupts every now and again from the screen. Today, for instance, the horoscope in the app on my phone tells me, "Soap operas are often a hyperbole on life's drama. It's getting tiresome, right? The only way to stop this annoyance is to refuse to participate, as you may play an integral role in keeping it going." Sure enough, I have to let go of someone and something this afternoon. So maybe the disciplines aren't incompatible after all. Taking the seer's advice, I can detach from the toxic norm and float so high, so far, that I am like a satellite in orbit, where I apprehend the televisual drama unfolding below not with affective intensity but rather with a kind of remote sensing, approaching (if not quite arriving) at scientific observation. And I am television, still.

---

23   Lisa Parks, *Cultures in Orbit: Satellites and the Televisual* (Durham: Duke University Press, 2005), 13.

22
September 22, 2018

Sutra

"We have, and will continue to process coming changes through our existing understandings of *television*. We will continue to call the increasingly large black boxes that serve as the focal point of our entertainment spaces *television* — regardless of how many boxes we need to connect to them in order to have the experience we desire or whether they are giant boxes or flat screens mounted on walls in the manner once reserved for art and decoration."[24]

Commentary

When *wasn't* television art and home décor? Think of all those luscious, baroque manifestations of television as furniture, populating the suburban living rooms of the Cold War. Perhaps because of the foreshortened scale in which they have dated, the television receivers of more recent history — those large black boxes of the late 1990s and early 2000s — are ironically quainter and goofier. If some of the television scales belong to Libra, I would like to weigh the large black box and the slim flat screen against each other. It is all right for those scales to tip markedly one way. After all, as Yoko Ono has it, "If you focus and lose balance, you fall. If you balance and lose focus, you die." Living as well as I may, I am keeping my eyes on the prize, the focal point of our entertainment spaces, and, as the teacher instructs me to do, I continue to call it *television*.

---

24 Amanda D. Lotz, *The Television Will Be Revolutionized* (New York: New York University Press, 2007), 21.

23
September 23, 2018

Sutra
"While the convergence of commercialism, popularity, and nonscripted television has clearly accelerated, much of what we call popular reality TV can be traced to existing formats and prior moments in U.S. television history."[25]

Commentary
When Adam Sandler told Bob Barker, "The price is wrong, bitch," he anticipated both the banal address that the host of *The Apprentice* would make to his costars and one that millions of us would now address to him in turn. Four years too late to sync with the moment at which we first learned what happens when people stop being polite and start getting real, two years too late to bite reality, Sandler was even further out of touch with one of television's *anni mirabiles,* the one in which it ate a Loud family. For my part, I am doing my best to make my trademark slogan, *I am a candid camera: I'm not kidding, I see shit.*

24
September 24, 2018

Sutra
"Certainly, I believe that the long-running and intensive debate about the 'adequacy to the real', the social sufficiency, of television's news and documentary portrayals is given a further, instructive point of reference by the photographic practices and the discourses of photographic comment that have been encouraged by digital platforms."[26]

---

25 Laurie Ouellette and Susan Murray, "Introduction," in *Reality TV: Remaking Television Culture,* eds. Susan Murray and Laurie Ouellette, 2nd edn. (New York: New York University Press, 2009), 4.

26 John Corner, "'Critical Social Optics' and the Transformations of Audio-Visual Culture," in *Relocating Television: Television in the Digital Context,* ed. Jostein Gripsrud (New York and London: Routledge, 2010), 52.

SUTURING "THE TV STUDIES SUTRAS"

Commentary
But what if I do not rise to the status of a candid camera? What if
I unwittingly introduce distortions to the sutras that I record? I
want to say, my words ringing in time with those of the evening
news anchor and of the voicing-over narrator in the television
documentary: *Trust me. Believe me.* As I do, I see an analogy between the relationship of television to digital photography and
the relationship of sutras to commentaries. I have a responsibility to the real and the true, but I also have the opportunity to
play, to unstick the "study" of "television study" from its more
typical forms of truth telling. Am I a camera obscura?

25
September 25, 2018

Sutra
"To say that Reality TV is rife with gender stereotypes is a bit like
shooting fish in a barrel."[27]

Commentary
I used to joke that "The Epistemology of Snooki" would make
a great name for an essay that would collide "high" theory with
a "low" object. But there is truth in jest. I would dearly love to
read that essay. Remember what I have been telling you all along
about the irreducible complexity to be found at every scale of
television? You only have to take a trip to *Jersey Shore* to discover as much.

27 Brenda R. Weber, "Introduction: Trash Talk: Gender as an Analytic on
    Reality Television," in *Reality Gendervision: Sexuality & Gender on Trans-
    atlantic Reality Television,* ed. Brenda R. Weber (Durham: Duke University
    Press, 2014), 8.

26
September 26, 2018

Sutra

"Mike's assurance to Edith seems apropos: 'Maybe we're not supposed to be understanding everything all at once. We need you.' This narrative refusal of closure and seeming acceptance of a gift of queer love that undoes sitcom timing results in a second close-up on Edith's face that, in my screening notes, I marked as lasting 'forever.' Maybe not quite, but almost."[28]

Commentary

Giver of this sutra, you are an adept at close reading, notwithstanding the footnote in which you point us to your screed against the practice. At the same time, close reading should not be autotelic, and it is not here. Maintaining the scale of close reading, the sutra also slips that scale in order to produce a constellation of (hear it two ways) moving parts: a theory of television time and its unraveling, a theory of the gift, a queer theory of love. If Edith's tears really could last forever, they would make us an ocean. Out of the bunker, into TV's wide, open waves.

27
September 27, 2018

Sutra

"Television can only enable identification within the parameters of its business models, and the business model of network television requires that representations be broadly legible and palatable."[29]

---

28   Amy Villarejo, *Ethereal Queer: Television, Historicity, Desire* (Durham: Duke University Press, 2014), 92.

29   F. Hollis Griffin, *Feeling Normal: Sexuality and Media Criticism in the Digital Age* (Bloomington and Indianapolis: Indiana University Press, 2016), 122.

Commentary
With reference to the previous sutra, we could call Edith's ditzy fluttering broadly legible, her fundamental kindness broadly palatable. But in the scene that said sutra describes, her tears in close-up render her otherwise, curious, special. It's that stranger Edith whom I crave to see whenever she might pop up. Ditto Will and Grace, Ellen, and whatever the name of the character John Goodman played in *Normal, Ohio.* Blink, and you'll miss these moments.

28
September 28, 2018

Sutra
"Indeed, one could go so far as to say that in the confrontation between receiver and animation, identifications, should they obtain, obtain as identifications *with* forms rather than *via* forms to putatively agential character/actors with suspect pretensions to rounded subjectivity."[30]

Commentary
A proto-queer and crypto-queer child of the eighties, I adored the protocols animating that queerest of TV cartoon crypts, *He-Man: Masters of the Universe.* Fast forward: an obliging consumer of neoliberalism's products, I wear a tee shirt on which He-Man and Skeletor are imaged — voguing. Its retailers advertise it with the tagline, "Eternia Is Burning." When I tried to share this detail with a friend, I made a Freudian slip and called Eternia *Eterna,* another super-queer zone of my youth, the underground city where a bunch of *One Life to Live*'s denizens were sent in unflattering hazmat-like suits. What can I tell you? Even cowgirls get the blues, and even gurus make mistakes. But if I wanted to sell you a tee shirt, a program, a bootleg DVD — the world — I would claim rather that my slip was not Freudian but

---

30 Nick Salvato, "Queer Structure, Animated Form, and *Really Rosie,*" *Camera Obscura* 33, no. 2 (2018): 139–59, at 154.

a brilliant example of sliding across television scales, starring partial constellations. After all, the slip takes the *I* out of Eternia, which also, paradoxically reemphasizes it and puts it back there: there, Etern(i)a, where I am the masters of the universe.

* * *

In an essay, "Citation Matters," that is well worth citing, cultural geographers Carrie Mott and Daniel Cockayne draw keen attention to the often under-attended politics of citation and the ways in which they matter:

> We argue for a conscientious engagement with the politics of citation that is mindful of how citational practices can be tools for either the reification of, or resistance to, unethical hierarchies of knowledge. Our approach is qualitative and conceptual, and offers a productive way to understand how citation can be rethought as a feminist and anti-racist technology. To ignore the politics of citation risks the continued hegemony of white heteromasculine knowledge production incongruous with the nuance and richness of other understandings of and perspectives on geographical phenomena.[31]

The salience of these observations not only to the study of "geographical phenomena" but also to scholarship writ large was very much on my mind during the period of my work on *Television Scales*. To be sure, Marilyn Strathern has enjoyed a highly successful and influential career, but she is not widely cited outside the discipline of anthropology. And she is certainly much less cited than theorists like Gilles Deleuze and Manuel DeLanda, from whose approaches I explicitly distinguish Strathern's in this book's introduction — in part because choosing to cite

---

31   Carrie Mott and Daniel Cockayne, "Citation Matters: Mobilizing the Politics of Citation toward a Practice of 'Conscientious Engagement,'" *Gender, Place & Culture* 24, no. 7 (2017): 954–73, at 956.

her in their stead constitutes my aim to honor and extend her feminism.

Similar to and, for this reason, connectable to Strathern, Bellamy is a writer who is widely admired in a number of circles. But they are smaller circles than the ones that laud — and cite, or devote critical essays and books to — other San Francisco-based novelists and poets; whenever in reading Bellamy I would encounter a confessional moment about the challenges of her somewhat precarious teaching life, I would think, for instance, of Lyn Hejinian's longstanding tenure at Berkeley. Devoting more sustained attention to Bellamy's work than has otherwise obtained in the scholarly humanities may, I hope, work to offset an imbalance in how we have been recognizing — or failing to recognize — the contributions of contemporary experimental writers.

Choosing to write sutras also makes Bellamy a candidate to connect, partially, to Strathern. As Bellamy reflects in the essayistic portion of her book, "Sutra literally means a thread or line that holds things together. It is derived from the verbal root siv-, meaning to sew. I think of embroidery, the precise knots and stitches my grandmother taught me to make flowers appear on pillowcases."[32] In other words, sutras themselves are connectors, and commentaries upon them partially extend their connective value and valences. Yet just as important to Bellamy's project as sutras and commentaries are the page breaks between one day's commentary and the next day's sutra, as well as the white spaces, small gaps, between various sections of her essay: namely, the sutures in which some artistic and intellective work, often not immediately or determinately nameable but nonetheless real and suggestive, is always getting accomplished — just as it is in Strathern's cuts. That is, sutures, or cuts, are not mere gaps but connectors in their own right, albeit connectors likelier to do the threading that they do in slippery and enigmatic ways. Perhaps that makes them not, as we might have expected, like the typical cuts used in television's camerawork — or even like tel-

---

32 Bellamy, *The TV Sutras*, 104–5.

evision's less typical, more pointed jump cuts — but rather like the second or so of black space that, on occasion, fills the screen right before a commercial break.

5

Coda

During the trip to Los Angeles that I invoked briefly in this book's third chapter, I not only conducted archival research at UCLA but also took a perverse, hours-long walk (every sustained pedestrian act is considered perverse by Angelenos) from my Airbnb in Westwood to the front of a house in Ladera Heights, recently used in location shooting to play the role of Amy Jellicoe's home's exterior in the brilliant but short-lived HBO series, *Enlightened*. At the time of planning and making this walk, I was referring half-jokingly to it in my notes as my effort in "vulgar psychogeography" — and that self-assessment still seems right to me, given how much less lost I got, following a route mostly down one broad avenue for a number of miles, and how much more instrumentalized the walk always already was (I was pretty certain that its inputs and outputs would feature in this book, as they do), than those wilder walks undertaken by British psychogeographers like Iain Sinclair. A vulgar walk has payoffs — including one partial answer to the question, raised earlier, about when and how television is watching us. If the question is posed in Los Angeles, then the answer might be writ in the outsized faces of Matthew Rhys and Keri Russell, or of "Andre the Giant," hovering over us in commercially slick billboards [see Figures 8 and

Fig. 8. *The Americans* are watching us. Photo by author.

Fig. 9. TV billboards are hovering giants. Photo by author.

Fig. 10. Lord, may Kiefer have been found. Photo by author.

9] — or, in a homemade sign, peering from the soulful eyes of a lost cat … who, this being LA, is named Kiefer [see Figure 10].

So I took pictures. And I used my phone to record observations in real time as I made my paces through the walk. Listening to the recording some time later — and having that familiarly defamiliarizing feeling of my own voice as uncanny — I pushed through the unease of the uncanny to decide on sharing two moments, inhabiting different scales and registers, from the ramble's rambling voicing:

(1) "When I decided this morning that I would indeed do this walk, I was conjuring in my mind a probably over-simplistic and over-binaristic opposition between the cramped enclosure of the study room in the basement of Powell Library and the possibility of experiencing a different sense of mobility and expansiveness through the contrasting, or what I took in my speculation about it to be contrasting, walk; but I think the better question might be: In what ways is there roominess in the small room designed for archival study and medita-

Fig. 11. God shines light on the *Enlightened* house. Photo by author.

tion, and how might a certain kind of walk produce enclo-
sures, alongside affordances? And, the yet better question,
following on the heels of that one, might be: What third term,
to be sort of deconstructive about it, might one introduce to
disrupt, rather than flip and flop, the terms *expansiveness/
roominess* and *cramped/enclosed?*"

(2) "Headquarters of Sony Pictures Entertainment face Studio
Royale Assisted Living here in Culver City, where I am seeing
quite a lot of octogenarians and nonagenarians. One woman
with a bedazzled hat was sitting at a bus stop, saw her friend
taking her afternoon stroll, and said, 'Isn't it lovely out today?' I think it is."

If the various forms of assaying that animate this book are working as I hope they may, then the word *scale* itself should, now,
come to mind as a strong candidate for the "third term" with
which to answer my putatively "better question." But to hope,
and to propose, as much is not to reify scale, not to claim for it

a singular dazzle like the beading on the old woman's hat, but to aim to demonstrate, one concluding time, its provisional value as one key concept among others with which to make partial constellations, starred with things as big as Sony headquarters and heady questions and as small as a quietly intoned remark about the loveliness of a day. (Those other concepts could range from lateness to satellite, or antenna to energy, and who knows what else besides.)

It was indeed lovely when I arrived at 5511 Senford Avenue in Ladera Heights. If she had taken the walk with me, I think Dodie Bellamy would have been as wryly amused as I was by the kitschy Christian light shining down, that afternoon, on the kitschy mid-century house [see Figure 11]. As much is suggested, anyway, by Bellamy's own cagy reference to *Enlightened* near the conclusion of *The TV Sutras:*

> A betrayal puts me in touch with my vulnerability, my brute confrontations with loss. I watch a DVD of a cultist with terminal cancer. She says her impending death is good for her practice because she really gets impermanence. She says she's happier than others around her because her eyes are wide open, drinking in the wonders of the world. Her eyes are painful to look at, bright yellow from jaundice. In the TV show *Enlightened,* the camera focuses on close-ups of brilliant roses to signal Laura Dern's moments of spiritual connection, calm. It's totally cheesy yet I recognize the feeling, where the gorgeousness of nature pops in sharp relief. Sometimes the glory of nature will expand to include nearby humans, sometimes not. In Developing the Novel my vision shifts and suddenly the students appear precious, all that life coursing through them, their tender hopes and fears. I feel like something in me has twirled open, kind of stoned. Back at home I'm sitting on the toilet facing Quincey, who is hunched over her bowl eating, and I can feel the life force

Fig. 12. Teola and I connect, partially. Photo by author.

coursing through her as well, and I think *We are programmed for ecstasy. Nobody owns that.*[1]

Tinier than the page breaks between one day's commentary and the next day's sutra, or than the small gaps between essay sections, the breath-like pauses between this passage's paratactically arranged sentences are also sutures, connectors. In a wonderful instance of her own way of making partial constellations, Bellamy demonstrates how to place together things as differently scaled as close-up roses from *Enlightened,* jaundiced eyes, pedagogy, loss, and the weird, feline pleasure that one of her cats takes from eating in the bathroom.

* * *

Back at home after my trip to Los Angeles, I'm sitting in bed and facing Teola, who is stretched out in blissful sleep [see Figure 12].

---

1   Dodie Bellamy, *The TV Sutras* (Brooklyn: Ugly Duckling Presse, 2014), 202–3.

Not particularly like either Marcel Proust or Barbara Cartland, I am not in the habit of writing in bed — and, before *Television Scales* changed my relationship to confession, I was even less in the habit of risking mortification by sharing personal details in my scholarly prose. But I do so, in a closing embroidery, to give you a sense — which is to say, a sensuousness — with which to understand texturally, dimensionally, the method not just of cogniting, but of phenomenally and fleshily igniting, a criticism, an aesthetics, of scalar attunement.

Bibliography

Allen, Robert C. "Introduction to the Second Edition, More Talk about TV." In *Channels of Discourse, Reassembled: Television and Contemporary Criticism,* edited by Robert C. Allen, 2nd edition, 1–20. New York: Routledge, 1992.

Amos, Tori "Pictures of You/The Big Picture - Washington, D.C." *YouTube,* August 16, 2014. https://youtu.be/XmGj25Y-O5NE.

Ang, Ien. *Watching Dallas: Soap Opera and the Melodramatic Imagination.* Translated by Della Couling. London and New York: Methuen, 1985.

Barthes, Roland. "Change the Object Itself." In *Image-Music-Text,* translated by Stephen Heath, 165–69. New York: Hill and Wang, 1977.

Bellamy, Dodie. *The TV Sutras.* Brooklyn: Ugly Duckling Presse, 2014.

Berry, Mary. "Mary Berry's Top 10 Baking Tips." *BBC Good Food.* http://www.bbcgoodfood.com/howto/guide/mary-berrys-top-10-baking-tips.

Brunsdon, Charlotte. "What Is the 'Television' of Television Studies?" In *The Television Studies Book,* edited by Christine Geraghty and David Lusted, 95–113. New York: St. Martin's Press, 1998.

Butler, Jeremy G. *Television Style*. New York: Routledge, 2010.

"Cakes." *The Great British Bake Off.* BBC Two. Original air date: August 17, 2010.

Cook, Kevin. *Flip: The Inside Story of TV's First Black Superstar*. New York: Viking, 2013.

Corner, John. "'Critical Social Optics' and the Transformation of Audio-Visual Culture." In *Relocating Television: Television in the Digital Context*, edited by Jostein Gripsrud, 41–54. New York and London: Routledge, 2010.

Crouch, Ian. "Looking for Meaning in 'Too Many Cooks.'" *The New Yorker*, November 10, 2014. http://www.newyorker.com/culture/culture-desk/connect-many-cooks.

"Daytime Soap Transcripts from the TV MegaSite." *The TV MegaSite*. http://tvmegasite.net/day/transcripts.shtml.

Dienst, Richard. *Still Life in Real Time: Theory after Television*. Durham: Duke University Press, 1994.

Doane, Mary Ann. "The Close-Up: Scale and Detail in the Cinema." *differences: A Journal of Feminist and Cultural Studies* 14, no. 3 (2003): 89–111. DOI: 10.1215/10407391-14-3-89.

Doty, Alexander. *Making Things Perfectly Queer: Interpreting Mass Culture*. Minneapolis: University of Minnesota Press, 1993.

Ellis, John. *Visible Fictions: Cinema, Television, Video*. Revised edition. New York: Routledge, 1992.

Esslin, Martin. *The Age of Television*. San Francisco: W.H. Freeman and Company, 1982.

Fiske, John, and John Hartley. *Reading Television*. London: Routledge, 2003.

"French Onion Soup," *The French Chef,* PBS. Original air date: February 9, 1963.

Friedberg, Anne. *The Virtual Window: From Alberti to Microsoft*. Cambridge: MIT Press, 2006.

Fuji Television Network, Inc. *Iron Chef: The Official Book*. Translated by Kaoru Hoketsu. New York: Berkeley Books, 2004.

Geraghty, Christine. "The Continuous Serial — A Definition." In *Coronation Street,* edited by Richard Dyer, 9–26. London: BFI, 1981.

Goldberg, Jessica. "The Era of the Ladder." *The Path,* Hulu. Original release date: March 30, 2016.

———. "What the Fire Throws." *The Path,* Hulu. Original release date: March 30, 2016.

Gray, Herman. *Watching Race: Television and the Struggle for Blackness.* Minneapolis: University of Minnesota Press, 2004.

Griffin, F. Hollis. *Feeling Normal: Sexuality and Media Criticism in the Digital Age.* Bloomington and Indianapolis: Indiana University Press, 2016.

Hargraves, Hunter. "(TV) Junkies in Need of an Intervention: On Addictive Spectatorship and Recovery Television." *Camera Obscura: Feminism, Culture, and Media Studies* 30, no. 1 (2015): 71–99. DOI: 10.1215/02705346-2885453.

Hartley, John. "The Real World of Audiences." In T*ele-ology: Studies in Television,* 119–25. London and New York: Routledge, 1992.

Holbraad, Martin, and Morten Axel Pedersen. "Planet M: The Intense Abstraction of Marilyn Strathern." *Anthropological Theory* 9, no. 4 (2009): 371–94. DOI: 10.1177/1463499609360117.

jacklalanneofficial. "The *Jack LaLanne* Full episode (Hangovers)." *YouTube,* January 17, 2016. https://youtu.be/tP4oRW-whoRw.

Jhally, Sut, and Justin Lewis. "Enlightened Racism: *The Cosby Show,* Audiences and the Myth of the American Dream." In *The Audience Studies Reader,* edited by William Brooker and Deborah Jermyn, 279–86. New York: Routledge, 2002.

Johnson, Patrick E. "'Quare' Studies, or (Almost) Everything I Know About Queer Studies I Learned from My Grandmother." *Text and Performance Quarterly* 21, no.1 (2001): 1–25. DOI: 10.1080/10462930128119.

Joyrich, Lynn. *Re-viewing Reception: Television, Gender, and Postmodern Culture.* Bloomington: Indiana University Press, 1996.

Kelly, Casper. "Too Many Cooks." Adult Swim. Original air date: October 28, 2014.

Landay, Lori. *I Love Lucy.* Detroit: Wayne State University Press, 2010.

Lotz, Amanda D. *The Television Will Be Revolutionized.* New York: New York University Press, 2007.

Maiellaro, Merrill, Khaki Jones, and Keith Crofford. "Spanish Translation." *Space Ghost Coast to Coast,* Cartoon Network. Original air date: April 15, 1994.

McCarthy, Anna. "From the Ordinary to the Concrete: Cultural Studies and the Politics of Scale." In *Questions of Method in Cultural Studies,* edited by Mimi White and James Schwoch, 21–53. Malden: Wiley-Blackwell, 2006.

Mellencamp, Patricia. "Prologue." In *Logics of Television: Essays in Cultural Criticism,* edited by Patricia Mellencamp, 1–13. Bloomington and Indianapolis: Indiana University Press, 1990.

Miller, Toby. "Preface." In *Television Studies,* edited by Toby Miller, vii. London: BFI, 2002.

Morley, David. *Television, Audiences and Cultural Studies.* London and New York: Routledge, 1992.

Morse, Margaret. "The Television News Personality and Credibility: Reflections on the News in Transition." In *Studies in Entertainment: Critical Approaches to Mass Culture,* edited by Tania Modleski, 55–79. Bloomington and Indianapolis: Indiana University Press, 1986.

Mott, Carrie, and Daniel Cockayne. "Citation Matters: Mobilizing the Politics of Citation toward a Practice of 'Conscientious Engagement.'" *Gender, Place & Culture: A Journal of Feminist Geography* 24, no. 7 (2017): 954–73. DOI: 10.1080/0966369X.2017.1339022.

Newcomb, Horace. *TV: The Most Popular Art.* Garden City: Anchor Press, 1974.

Oullette, Laurie. *Lifestyle TV.* New York: Routledge, 2016.

———, and Susan Murray. "Introduction." In *Reality TV: Remaking Television Culture,* edited by Susan Murray and Laurie Oullette, 2nd edition, 1–20. New York: New York University Press, 2009.

Parks, Lisa. *Cultures in Orbit: Satellites and the Televisual.* Durham: Duke University Press, 2005.

Polan, Dana. *Julia Child's* The French Chef. Durham: Duke University Press, 2011.

Powter, Susan. "Stop the Insanity." USA NETWORK for syndication. Original broadcast: 1993.

Rasmussen, Kayti Sweetland. "Father of Fitness." *Pachofa-Unfinished* (blog), March 7, 2015. http://pachofaunfinished. wordpress.com/2015/03/07/father-of-fitness/.

Salvato, Nick. *Obstruction.* Durham: Duke University Press, 2016.

———. "Queer Structure, Animated Form, and Really Rosie." In *Camera Obscura: Feminism, Culture, and Media Studies* 33, no. 2 (2018): 139–59. DOI: 10.1215/02705346-6923142.

"Season 8 Premiere," Flip or Flop, HGTV. Original air date: May 31, 2018.

Shapiro, Irwin. *Felix on Television: "A Flip-It Book."* New York: Wonder Books, 1956.

Shattuc, Jane M. "The Oprahfication of America: Talk Shows and the Public Sphere." In *Television, History, and American Culture: Feminist Critical Essays,* edited by Mary Beth Haralovich and Lauren Rabinovitz, 168–80. Durham: Duke University Press, 1999.

Silver, Stu. "Lizards Ain't Snakes," *Brothers,* Showtime. Original air date: August 23, 1984.

Smith-Shomade, Beretta. *Shaded Lives: African-American Women and Television.* New Brunswick: Rutgers University Press, 2002.

Spigel, Lynn. "Introduction." In *Television after TV: Essays on a Medium in Transition,* edited by Lynn Spigel and Jan Olsson, 1–40. Durham: Duke University Press, 2004.

Steimatsky, Noa. *The Face on Film.* New York: Oxford University Press, 2017.

Strathern, Marilyn. "Environments Within: An Ethnographic Commentary on Scale." In *Culture, Landscape, and the Environment: The Linacre Lectures 1997*, edited by Kate Flint and Howard Morphy, 44–71. Oxford: Oxford University Press, 2000.

———. *Partial Connections*. Updated edition. New York: AltaMira Press, 2004.

———. *The Relation: Issues in Complexity and Scale*. Cambridge: Prickly Pear Press, 1995.

Sullivan, Robert David. "Enjoy the Sensual Delights of Cooking with 10 Episodes of Julia Child's *The French Chef*." *The AV Club*, November 21, 2012. http://tv.avclub.com/enjoy-the-sensual-delights-of-cooking-with-10episodes-1798234736.

Sutherland, Meghan. *The Flip Wilson Show*. Detroit: Wayne State University Press, 2008.

"The New Orleans House." *This Old House*, PBS. Original air date: February 1, 1991.

"The Wayland House." *This Old House*, PBS. Original air date: November 30, 1991.

Travis, Sean. "Life's a Snore." *Roseanne's Nuts*, Lifetime. Original air date: July 20, 2011.

VanDerWerff, Todd. "Why the Internet Is Obsessed with 'Too Many Cooks'." *Vox*, November 11, 2014. http://www.vox.com/2014/11/11/7191255/too-many-cooks-explained-what-is.

Villarejo, Amy. "Adorno by the Pool; or, Television Then and Now." *Social Text* 34, no. 2 (2016): 71–87, DOI: 10.1215/01642472-3467978.

———. *Ethereal Queer: Television, Historicity, Desire*. Durham: Duke University Press, 2014.

Weber, Brenda R. "Introduction: Trash Talk: Gender as an Analytic on Reality Television." In *Reality Gendervision: Sexuality & Gender on Transatlantic Reality Television*, edited by Brenda R. Weber, 1–33. Durham: Duke University Press, 2014.

Westergaard, John, and Henrietta Resler. *Class in a Capitalist Society: A Study of Contemporary Britain*. Harmondsworth: Penguin, 1976.

White, Mimi. *Tele-Advertising: Therapeutic Discourse in American Television.* Chapel Hill: University of North Carolina Press, 1992.

Williams, Raymond. *Television: Technology and Cultural Form.* London and New York: Routledge Classics, 1974.

Wollheim, Bruno, dir. *In Your Face:* "Dame Marilyn Strathern (2001), by Daphne Todd." Coluga Pictures for Channel 4, 2002.

www.ingramcontent.com/pod-product-compliance
Lightning Source LLC
Chambersburg PA
CBHW050654270326
41927CB00012B/3025

* 9 7 8 1 9 5 0 1 9 2 4 1 0 *